Fun Puppet Skits
for
Schools and Libraries

Fun Puppet Skits
for
Schools and Libraries

JOANNE F. SCHROEDER

1995
TEACHER IDEAS PRESS
A Division of
Libraries Unlimited, Inc.
Englewood, Colorado

To my mother, Frances Jirik Johnson, who read to me.

✳

Copyright © 1995 Joanne F. Schroeder
All Rights Reserved
Printed in the United States of America

TEACHER IDEAS PRESS
A Division of Libraries Unlimited, Inc.
P.O. Box 6633
Englewood, CO 80155-6633
1-800-237-6124

Production Editor: Jason Cook
Copy Editor: Ramona Gault
Typesetting and Interior Design: Kay Minnis
Photographs and Illustrations: Joanne F. Schroeder

Library of Congress Cataloging-in-Publication Data

Schroeder, Joanne F.
    Fun puppet skits for schools and libraries / Joanne F. Schroeder.
    xvi, 121 p. 22x28 cm.
    Includes indexes.
    ISBN 1-56308-298-5
    1. Puppet plays. 2. Puppet theater in education. 3. Libraries
and puppets.
PN1980.S37   1995
812'.54--dc20   95-37221
                                                          CIP

Contents

vi / Contents

Preface

Bringing together in printed form the many puppet skits I have developed during my years in puppetry has been a challenge. I was working as a children's librarian when I joined the Greater Houston Puppetry Guild in order to learn the art of puppetry. I wanted to perform puppet skits based on books to enhance the library story time. I felt that puppetry could stimulate children's interest in reading a book that was presented to them in a puppet performance. My search started in the library for the right book to dramatize in a puppet skit. Evenings and weekends were used to create the puppet skit—that is, write down the action of the skit and make or buy the puppets needed.

After I had been in the Puppetry Guild for several months, I realized that puppet shows are time-consuming productions, with puppets to be made, a stage to be built, scripts and music to be written, and much rehearsal to be done, along with lights and a sound system for production. At this point I still wanted to do puppetry but felt that I needed to do it more efficiently. Consequently, I developed short puppet skits, based on picture books, that could be performed quickly without elaborate staging, props, and rehearsals.

When I find a story that lends itself to puppetry, I write the script, or select the music if it is to be performed to music, and then buy or make the puppets. If I cannot make a puppet I need, and I cannot find it in a store, I substitute another puppet until I find the right one. For example, in the skit "Sody Sallyraytus" I needed a mean-looking bear. All I could find was a silly-looking one, which I used for years. At a national puppet festival I saw the mean-looking bear I needed in the puppetry exchange and bought it. Sources for ready-made puppets include toy stores, gift shops, children's bookstores, nature stores, puppet festivals, thrift stores, and arts and crafts fairs.

The book on which I base a puppet skit must be one that can be performed easily and quickly. As a librarian, I find that I cannot devote large amounts of time to the puppet theater. Therefore, the performances are short, with no scenery and few if any props. Then I practice the performance several times before presenting it to a class. In the school library, I present the puppet performance to several hundred children during the course of a week (this can require as many as 20 presentations). After that much practice, I know the script and movements of the puppets quite well.

I store the entire puppet skit in a bag and hang it in a closet. This way it is ready for the next year—when I pick up the bag of puppets for a performance, a quick glance at the puppets and script is all I need before presentation. Basically, as long as I remember the sequence of events in the skit, little or no rehearsal time is needed. For example, for the skit "The Old Lady Who Swallowed a Fly," the old lady puppet and the finger puppets that go into her tummy are placed in a bag, along with a paper or audiocassette copy of the song. The next time I want to perform this skit, I can pick up the bag and know that everything required for the performance is there. This saves time that might be spent looking for a tape or puppet.

The Puppetry Guild meetings featured workshops by various puppeteers. Each had a specialty, and I tried to learn about all of the many types of puppetry that were offered. Consequently, this book features hand puppets, rod puppets, shadow puppets, black light puppetry, stretch-neck puppets, ventriloquist dummies, finger puppets, arm puppets, yarn dolls, and marionettes. I found out that most professional puppeteers make their own puppets. I also found out that I do not have the talent to make puppets other than simple finger puppets. Fortunately for us teachers and librarians, many stores carry puppets, so we can buy what we need. Do not let what you cannot do hinder what you can do. Buy the puppets you need if you cannot make them.

Large cities (populations of 1 million or more) have puppet guilds. If you live in a large city, take advantage of the puppet guild to learn the art of puppetry. If you do not live in a large city, attend one of the annual puppet festivals held in the United States, sponsored by the Puppeteers of America. Membership in the Puppeteers of America brings a quarterly puppetry journal and information about the annual festivals. (For membership information, write to: Puppeteers of America, Membership Office, #5 Cricklewood Path, Pasadena, CA 91107.)

During the early 1970s I worked in libraries in the Brevard County School System in Florida. My next position was with the Friendswood Public Library in Friendswood, Texas, as children's librarian. In the 1980s I became a school librarian working in elementary schools in the Pasadena Independent School District in Pasadena, Texas. In the 1990s I joined the faculty at McAdams Junior High School in Dickinson, Texas. My puppetry began in earnest in the elementary schools and continues in the junior high schools, where puppet skits are presented to reading classes and to special education students. My puppetry skills are also used to give booktalks.

In junior high school, Miss Kitty, a hand puppet, helps me give booktalks on books about romance, books in which girls are the main characters. Miss Kitty likes boys, and I keep her in character as she reacts to my telling about the books. She might ask one of the boys in the class to take her fishing when I say that a girl's boyfriend took her out to eat. Jake the Cowboy, a ventriloquist dummy, helps me give booktalks on books in which boys who like or date girls are the main characters. Jake the Cowboy likes girls. He can raise his eyebrows, extend his hand, and make comments about holding the hand of a girl who is in the class. The students always ask me to bring Jake back another time.

For booktalks, I also use my ability to make different faces, as I do in the skit "The Principal." I pretend that I am a character from a book and tell students about the book from this character's point of view. Presenting booktalks in this manner gets students' attention and heightens their interest in reading. It also creates a bond between me and the students.

Puppetry has given me the opportunity to discover my uniqueness through creativity. I have learned that the use of humor in drama is extremely important to me. Thus, when creating story lines for fairy tales such as "The Three Little Pigs," "Cinderella," and "Goldilocks and the Three Bears," I use humorous lines. Humor is an effective device for engaging students. As they react to the traditional story lines with laughter, students develop an experiential understanding of *sequence*.

This book can help you make puppets come alive in your classroom or library. Imagine that the song "Old MacDonald Had a Farm" is playing. Children have puppets on their hands and smiles of delight on their faces as they listen and move to the music—actively involved in their own learning—performing a puppet show with their friends and classmates.

One memorable puppet skit that got a tremendous laugh was a performance of "Don't Bother Me." One of the children in the room insisted on standing right in front of the puppet stage no matter how many times he was asked to sit down. When the monster suddenly came up out of the stage and flew into his face, he ducked and ran to the back of the room. No one could get that child to sit down except the puppet.

Acknowledgments

I wish to thank the following libraries for their support: Friendswood Public Library, Friendswood, Texas; Helen Hall Library, League City, Texas; Pasadena Public Library, Pasadena, Texas; Mares Memorial Library, Dickinson, Texas; Genevieve Miller Hitchcock Public Library, Hitchcock, Texas; and Pearland Public Library, Pearland, Texas. They supported my work by providing a place to do research and a place to perform puppet skits and conduct puppet workshops. They have funded other puppeteers, puppet shows, and puppet workshops as well, including some of the shows and workshops presented by the Greater Houston Puppetry Guild.

I wish to thank my husband, Syd Schroeder, for the many hours he spent formatting this book. His computer skills, editing skills, and dedication to the project helped make this book a reality.

I wish to thank all the librarians and teachers who have attended my workshops over the years. They accepted my work as worthwhile and they became my fans, attending my workshops year after year. Thank you for your support and encouragement.

I wish to thank the Puppeteers of America for providing puppet festivals across the United States. Their dedication to this art has helped many improve their puppetry skills.

Finally, I wish to thank the Greater Houston Puppetry Guild for providing me with the opportunity to learn the art of puppetry.

Introduction

Most puppet books tell you how to make puppets. This book tells you how to use puppets. It is intended to promote reading, for the puppet skits are based on books and songs. You and the children enjoy your puppet shows through laughter, togetherness, smiles, and sighs. Yes, try on a puppet for sighs.

This book was written with the busy librarian and teacher in mind. Each puppet skit suggests subjects around which your story time or lesson can be centered (a skit subject index is included). Suggested books for you to read to the class, related to the subject of the skit, are listed (an author/title index is included). If you have favorite books of your own, read them, too. During a 30-minute story time in the library, I read a book, perform a puppet skit, and sing and play the guitar. For example, for a story time on the subject of dogs, I might read the book *Mine Will, Said John* by Helen Griffith, perform the skit "Doggie in the Window," and sing the song "Bingo" (the skit "Doggie in the Window" is my personal favorite: during a performance of this skit, children in the audience often tell each other that the puppet is a real dog). Each skit also includes a list of required materials as well as a setup procedure.

Selecting Stories

The number of characters and the amount of action in the story are the two determining factors in choosing a book for a puppet skit. If the skit is to be performed by one person, ideal books are those with one or two characters. A puppeteer working alone can use a story with more than two characters if you can arrange it so that several characters are not onstage at the same time. Also, you can use a puppet's voice onstage while the puppet is offstage to reduce the number of puppets visible at one time.

If you need more than two characters onstage at the same time, you might use a tandem device such as a wooden stick with another wooden stick attached crosswise. Several puppets can then be attached to the crosswise stick. For example, this can be done in the skit "The Three Little Pigs" to put all three pigs onstage at one time, using just one hand.

A puppet skit needs a substantial amount of action. All dialog and no action can make for a very dull performance.

When creating skits that are based on books, be advised that if you intend to perform the skit professionally (i.e., a performance for which you receive a fee), you should seek written permission from whomever holds the copyright before doing so.

Selecting Music

If you are performing within an institution (school, library, hospital) or a theme park, and you are using commercially available recordings, technically you should be covered by that facility's BMI, ASCAP, or SESAC performance license. These annual licenses are granted to such facilities allowing them to perform musical selections. Entertainment facilities such as hotels, restaurants, and cruise ships also use such licenses. It is the institution's responsibility to obtain these licenses. You are not liable if you are hired to perform in a facility that does not have these licenses.

If you are using commercially available music for a production that will be filmed or videotaped for distribution, you must obtain a synchronization license from the owner of the recording or the owner's agent.

If you use a commercial recording of a public domain tune, a synchronization license is also necessary. For example, if you wish to use the arrangement of a tune recorded by Arthur Fiedler and the Boston Pops on RCA Victor Records, you would need to obtain a synchronization license from the copyright owner for that specific arrangement of the public domain tune. Again, this applies if your performance is for broadcast, video recording/release, or theatrical distribution. However, if you create and record your own version of John Philip Sousa's "Stars and Stripes Forever," a synchronization license would not be needed, as the tune is in the public domain. The synchronization license is also needed if you intend to sell videocassette copies of your puppet show for profit.

There are no set fees for music clearance. Whatever the record company or copyright owner thinks they can get is what is charged. A higher fee is charged for more current or popular recordings.

Please use these guidelines at your own risk. I encourage educators to order their own copy of a recording (making copies of a recording is a violation of copyright law). If you intend to perform a skit professionally (i.e., a performance for which you will receive a fee), you should seek written permission from whomever holds the copyright before doing so. If you have any questions regarding the legalities of your use of others' materials, seek professional advice.

Performing Puppet Skits

Because this is quick and easy puppetry, there is no scenery and there are relatively few props. Many of the puppet skits do not require a stage. Skits that involve just the puppeteer pantomiming the actions include "Doggie in the Window," "Grandma's Glasses," and "The Old Lady Who Swallowed a Fly." Skits that involve the audience in pantomiming the actions include "Old MacDonald Had a Farm," "The Little Red Hen," "April Rabbits," and "The Nutcracker and the Mouse King."

The song "The Hokey Pokey" lends itself to an easy puppet performance: a marionette dance (the children can dance right along with the marionette—that is, "put their right foot in, put their right foot out," and so on). Another quick and easy storytelling device is a glove puppet, with all the characters in the story attached to a glove. In this book I give several ideas for performing folktales and fairytales using glove puppets, including a flannel board version of "Cinderella."

Commercially manufactured puppets, readily available in most toy stores, are suitable for use in the skits described in this book. The appendix contains directions for making rod puppets, sock puppets, yarn dolls, and marionettes.

Directions for making a portable, folding puppet stage are provided on page xvi. As a matter of note, the terms *stage right* and *stage left* refer to the right and left sides of the stage as seen from the puppeteer's perspective when standing inside the stage. The term *playboard* refers to the part of the stage on which the puppets "stand." A *scrim* is a sheet of cloth that permits one-way viewing (the puppeteer can see the audience, but the audience cannot see the puppeteer).

Puppet Voices

Puppet voices are an important part of the puppet skit. An effective voice must come from the puppet's character. Think about the character and how you can bring it to life through the voice you give the puppet. Use variations in the four basic voice characteristics—pitch, placement, speech patterns, and voice quality—to define the puppet through its voice.

PITCH

Voices can be made different by changing the pitch: low, medium, high, falsetto. The intended age of the character will be a guide to the correct pitch. An old man would have a voice with a low pitch. A witch or a young child might have a falsetto voice.

PLACEMENT

Placement refers to producing voice sounds in different areas of your body to create different sound characteristics. Your voice can be produced through your nose, the back of your mouth, the front of your mouth, your chest, and your back.

SPEECH PATTERNS

Speech patterns contribute to a puppet's unique character. Southern, hillbilly, or foreign accents, or repetitive use of certain phrases, will make a character identifiable to the audience even when it is speaking offstage.

VOICE QUALITY

Vary your voice quality. This is the color that helps the audience experience the event. Volume (soft, medium, loud, erratic) and speed (slow, medium, fast, rhythmic) are components of voice quality. Give your voice enough force for the audience to hear the puppet talk. If you find that you have given the wrong voice to a puppet, change it. Do not change it in the middle of the show, but by the next show make sure that the puppet has a new voice.

To find the right voice for your puppet character, think about what the puppet is like: shy or outgoing, happy or sad, boastful or bashful, "nerdy" or sophisticated, smart or confused, nervous or relaxed, young or old. Then think about how the character would react in different situations. Choose a voice that is comfortable for you, so that you are not strained by its use.

The puppet's movements, in combination with the right voice, can create a realistic character. Using a certain amount of exaggeration creates a unique stage presence. Timing is important in your delivery of speech and movement. Be consistent with the puppet's voice and character.

Keep trying to improve the quality of your puppets' voices. This is always possible with live puppet shows, as opposed to recorded ones.

VENTRILOQUISM

Begin learning ventriloquism by singing the "A B C" song. Sing with your lips apart, relaxed and not moving, and your teeth slightly apart. The ventriloquist's voice is produced without moving your lips, but you do need air to speak, so keep your mouth slightly open. There are a few letters that are difficult to pronounce this way, but you can substitute easier sounds for them: B = "D" sound, F = "eth" sound, M = "N" sound, P = "T" sound, and V = "thee" sound.

Bs and Ps are the hardest to pronounce because these letters are "plosive" sounds. (*Plosive* means "explosive." Ventriloquists talk by forming words inside the mouth and saying them without moving the lips, which helps to form the explosive sounds.) To substitute the letter D for B, notice that the letter D is pronounced with the tip of your tongue on the roof of your mouth. To get a more realistic B sound, slide the tip of your tongue forward, so it is just behind your teeth. Flatten out your tongue on the roof of your mouth, and pull your tongue backward. Substitute T for the letter P. The plosive sounds B and P sound better if you pause before speaking them.

To create a believable M using the substitute letter N, you need to vibrate the letter. With the letter N, the tip of your tongue is on the roof of your mouth. To make this into M, flatten your tongue against the roof of your mouth. Say the word "nary," and it should sound like "Mary."

The term "throwing your voice" comes from the illusion you create. It looks like the puppet is actually talking. To create this illusion, your hand needs to open and close the dummy's mouth for each syllable, in coordination with what your lips would do if you were moving them. A television set has sound coming from speakers. Yet we believe the sound comes from the person who is talking on the screen because his or her mouth is moving.

A good place to practice ventriloquism is while you are driving your car. Either practice a routine or sing along to the songs on the car radio.

Hand Puppet Manipulation

When putting a puppet on your hand, you have some choice as to where your fingers will be inside the puppet. First, your thumb is always in a puppet hand. Second, your forefinger is always in the puppet head. Third (this is where the choice comes in), you may insert your middle finger in the puppet head along with your forefinger, if there is room, and place your ring finger and pinkie in the puppet's other hand. You could also put your pinkie by itself in the puppet's other hand, folding the middle and ring fingers down out of the way. Choose the position most comfortable for you.

When working with puppets onstage, keep them standing erect. Lack of concentration and tiredness cause puppets to lean over or sink. You must concentrate on an imaginary floor. Rely on the strength of your arm to hold the puppet up, not on the playboard. Do not lean on the playboard.

To keep the puppet upright and the strength in your arm, keep your elbow directly under your puppet as it walks and talks on stage. When the puppet talks and acts, move it. Do not move it when it is not acting. When a puppet is moving around while another puppet is acting onstage, it is upstaging the puppet that is supposed to be getting the attention of the audience.

ARM MOVEMENTS

Walk: Move the puppet across the playboard. There are many different ways to walk.

Sit down: Lean the puppet forward, lower it, then straighten it.

Get up: Lean forward, lift up, and straighten puppet, moving the seat up first and the head last.

Fall down: Puppet falls forward, backward, or in a heap.

Laugh, cry, snore, and sneeze: These can be big body movements from your elbow with loud sounds.

WRIST MOVEMENTS

Say "no": Turn the whole puppet from side to side with your wrist.

Look (up, down, around): Puppet should look at other characters or the audience, not at the ceiling or floor, unless the script calls for it.

Bow: Drop your hand down and bring it up again.

Laugh, cry, snore, and sneeze: Use your wrist for "medium-size" action with "medium-size" sounds.

FINGER MOVEMENTS

Say "yes": Bend your fingers in the puppet's head for a nod.

Wave: When the puppet is saying good-bye, wave your pinkie or thumb.

Think: Tap or scratch the puppet's head with your pinkie or thumb inserted into the puppet's hand.

Point: With your pinkie or thumb in the puppet's hand, point to another character.

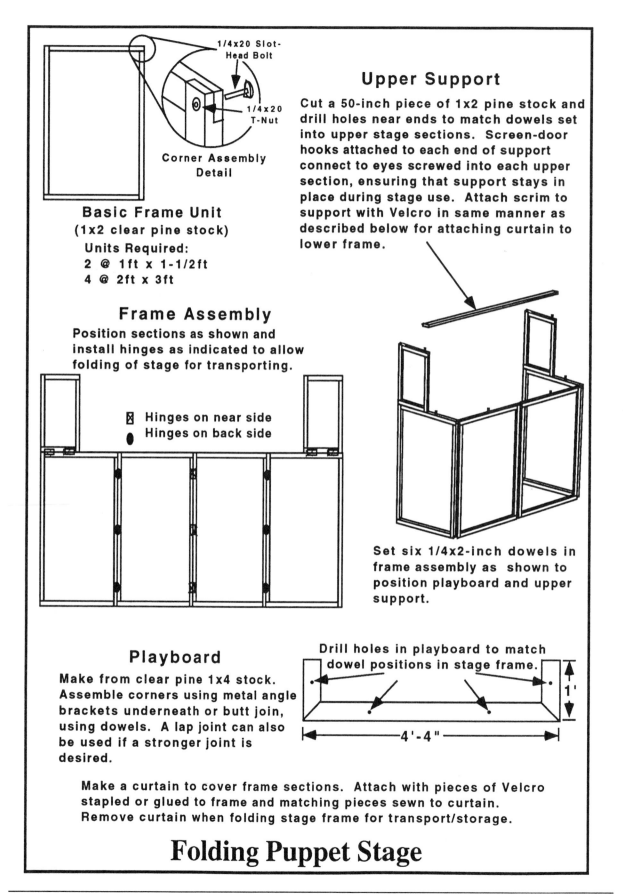

1/4x20 Slot-Head Bolt

1/4x20 T-Nut

Corner Assembly Detail

Upper Support

Cut a 50-inch piece of 1x2 pine stock and drill holes near ends to match dowels set into upper stage sections. Screen-door hooks attached to each end of support connect to eyes screwed into each upper section, ensuring that support stays in place during stage use. Attach scrim to support with Velcro in same manner as described below for attaching curtain to lower frame.

Basic Frame Unit
(1x2 clear pine stock)

Units Required:
2 @ 1ft x 1-1/2ft
4 @ 2ft x 3ft

Frame Assembly

Position sections as shown and install hinges as indicated to allow folding of stage for transporting.

☒ Hinges on near side
● Hinges on back side

Set six 1/4x2-inch dowels in frame assembly as shown to position playboard and upper support.

Playboard

Make from clear pine 1x4 stock. Assemble corners using metal angle brackets underneath or butt join, using dowels. A lap joint can also be used if a stronger joint is desired.

Drill holes in playboard to match dowel positions in stage frame.

1'

4'-4"

Make a curtain to cover frame sections. Attach with pieces of Velcro stapled or glued to frame and matching pieces sewn to curtain. Remove curtain when folding stage frame for transport/storage.

Folding Puppet Stage

Part I

CHILDREN'S BOOKS / NEW THEMES

Adventures in Baby-Sitting

SUBJECT: Safety / Monsters

BOOKS TO READ:
The Chick and the Duckling by Mirra Ginsburg (Macmillan, 1972).
Abiyoyo by Pete Seeger (Macmillan, 1986).
The Very Worst Monster by Pat Hutchins (Mulberry Books, 1985).

MATERIALS: Rod puppet: girl; yarn doll: Johnny; monster sock puppets: two different monsters; car silhouette; dowel; broom holder; hand puppet stage.

SETUP: Place Johnny, the yarn doll, on the playboard at stage left. Holding the girl rod puppet with your left hand, position it near the yarn doll. Attach the broom holder to the side of the playboard (facing you) at stage left. Attach the dowel to the car silhouette and place it into the broom holder. Place one of the monster sock puppets on your right hand and hold it at stage right (your thumb and your forefinger are the arms that pick up the yarn doll).

THE SHOW

GIRL.
Hurry up, Mom. I don't want to sit in a hot car all day baby-sitting. I wonder what is taking her so long. [*She looks to the right.*] There is a monster in that store window. I have to get a closer look.

[*She walks over to the monster.*] Hey, Mr. Monster, can you turn around? [*Turn monster to the right and to the left.*] Mr. Monster, can you jump up and down? [*Move monster to jump up and down.*] Can you take a bow? [*Move monster to bow.*] Wow, this is more fun than having a baby brother. Baby brother? Oops, I almost forgot about my baby brother!

[*She runs across the stage to the yarn doll.*] Johnny? Johnny, are you all right? You look terrible. [*She picks up the yarn doll.*] Somebody help me! My brother is sick! [*She runs offstage. Put her down backstage. Grasp the rod on the car silhouette and move the monster over to the car.*]

MONSTER.
Monster drive car. Monster drive car. [*Make an engine noise as you move the monster and the car to stage right and offstage. Then make the sound of a crash. Bring the girl rod puppet onstage without the yarn doll Johnny.*]

GIRL.
Johnny is going to be just fine. Now where is our car? It was right here a minute ago. What happened to our car? The monster took it? I got in trouble over my baby brother because of that monster, and now I'll get in trouble over the car because of that monster. No more monsters for me. [*She exits. Enter another monster puppet looking around.*]

MONSTER.
Seen any girls around here lately? [*He exits.*]

Discuss with the audience safety procedures that the baby-sitter ignored (e.g., don't leave children alone in cars).

Amy Armadillo

SUBJECT: Litter / Travel / Nature

BOOKS TO READ:
The Journey Home by Alison Lester (Houghton Mifflin, 1991).
John Tabor's Ride by Edward C. Day (Alfred A. Knopf, 1989).
The Wartville Wizard by Don Madden (Macmillan, 1986).

MATERIALS: Hand puppet: armadillo; props: blue bonnet hat, Blue Bonnet Margarine box, bluebonnet flower, crumpled balls of paper; stage: box that can be used as a "jeep" prop—gift box from a clothing store or some other suitable container from which the puppet can perform.

SETUP: Make the puppet (you need to be able to push the puppet into the container stage, grasp objects with the armadillo's legs, and bring them out "easily"). Place the puppet and props into the container stage.

THE SHOW

The Texas state flower is the bluebonnet. In this puppet skit, an armadillo, an animal native to Texas, is asked if she has any bluebonnets in her jeep. She pulls out two kinds of "blue bonnets" before she finally gets the right one. Then she starts throwing trash. The audience enjoys this part, and it provides an opportunity to mention a motto in Texas, "Don't mess with Texas!"

YOU.
Amy, I've seen many armadillos along the side of the road. I wonder what happened to them? Rrrrrooom! Bonk! That's what I was afraid of. Something else I see along the side of the road are bluebonnets. Do you have any bluebonnets in your jeep?

ARMADILLO.
[*She nods head yes.*]

YOU.
Could we see them?

ARMADILLO.
[*She goes into jeep and brings out a blue bonnet hat.*]

YOU.
I don't mean the kind of blue bonnet you wear, I mean the kind you see along the side of the road.

ARMADILLO.
[*She reaches into the jeep and brings out an empty Blue Bonnet Margarine box.*]

YOU.
That is garbage. [*To audience:*] What do we mean when we ask for bluebonnets?

AUDIENCE.
Flowers.

ARMADILLO.
[*She reaches into jeep and brings out a bluebonnet flower.*]

YOU.
[*To audience:*] Why are they special in Texas?

AUDIENCE.
They are the Texas state flower.

YOU.
Amy, do you have a trash bag in there?

ARMADILLO.
[*She nods head no.*]

YOU.
You don't know? Look for one.

ARMADILLO.
[*She reaches into the jeep and throws out a wad of paper.*]

YOU.

Amy, we are at the [*name the place*].
They keep it very clean here. Don't
throw things on the floor. Now, look for
a trash bag.

ARMADILLO.

[*She throws out a fake rock.*]

YOU.

Say, didn't you ever hear of "Don't Mess
with Texas!"?

ARMADILLO.

[*She shakes head no.*]

YOU.

What did you hear?

ARMADILLO.

[*She whispers into your ear.*]

YOU.

If you don't want it anymore, throw it
on the floor!

ARMADILLO.

[*She whispers into your ear.*]

YOU.

Okay. Just put all this stuff back in the
jeep. We will go to the store for trash
bags.

ARMADILLO.

[*She throws the Blue Bonnet Margarine
box onto the floor.*]

YOU.

[*To audience:*] Excuse me, I'm taking
her to the store. Amy, be good. Wave
good-bye. [*Pick up the margarine box
and exit.*]

This puppet skit can be adapted to
other puppets and containers. The following is a suggestion for a snowman hand
puppet and a plastic flower pot container:

YOU.

Snowball, I see you and your ice bucket
have come down to Texas for the winter.

PUPPET.

[*It nods yes.*]

YOU.

In Texas we have bluebonnets that are
very special. Do you know what a
bluebonnet is?

PUPPET.

[*It nods yes.*]

YOU.

You do?

PUPPET.

[*It whispers in your ear.*]

YOU.

You found a bluebonnet along the side
of the road?

PUPPET.

[*It nods yes.*]

YOU.

I can't believe it. Let me see.

PUPPET.

[*It reaches into container and pulls out
a blue bonnet hat.*]

YOU.

That is not the kind of bluebonnet we
mean. Usually you find these in people's
houses. We mean the kind of bluebonnet
that you would find outside along the
side of the road.

PUPPET.

[*It pulls out an empty Blue Bonnet
Margarine box.*]

YOU.

This is garbage. This is an empty box
from Blue Bonnet Margarine. What do
we mean, boys and girls, when we say
bluebonnets?

AUDIENCE.

Flowers.

YOU.

Do you have any flowers in there?

PUPPET.

[*It nods yes, reaches into container, and
pulls out a bluebonnet flower.*]

Follow the rest of the skit as written
for "Amy Armadillo."

Ape Face

SUBJECT: School / Monkeys / Food

BOOKS TO READ:
Five Little Monkeys Sitting in a Tree by Eileen Christelow (Clarion Books, 1991).
Monkey in the Middle by Eve Bunting (Harcourt Brace Jovanovich, 1984).
Born in the Gravy by Denys Cazet (Orchard Books, 1993).

MATERIALS: Hand puppet: monkey; props: paper lunch bag or lunch box, plastic fruit: purple grapes, red apple, yellow lemon, yellow banana.

SETUP: Put the plastic fruit into the bag or lunch box and place it on your lap. Put the monkey puppet on your hand.

THE SHOW

YOU.
Hi, Ape Face! What's in the bag?

MONKEY.
[*It whispers in your ear.*]

YOU.
You brought your lunch to school. What are you having for lunch?

MONKEY.
[*It whispers in your ear.*]

YOU.
A yellow banana? These boys and girls know what a yellow banana looks like. They want to see your yellow banana.

MONKEY.
[*It responds by sticking its head into the bag and pulling out a bunch of purple grapes in its mouth.*]

YOU.

That's not a yellow banana. Those are purple grapes. What happened?

MONKEY.

[*It whispers in your ear as you respond.*]

YOU.

You grabbed the wrong thing? [*Set the grapes aside as you respond.*] Why, I never grab the wrong thing. [*Glance at the monkey, which is nodding its head in an affirmative manner.*] Well, sometimes I do. You want to try again? [*Monkey nods yes.*]

MONKEY.

[*It puts its head in the bag again, and this time pulls out a red apple.*]

YOU.

That's not a yellow banana. That is a red apple. What happened this time?

MONKEY.

[*It whispers in your ear.*]

YOU.

You forgot what you went after? Why, I never forget what I go after. [*Take the apple, set it aside, and look back at the monkey.*] Well, sometimes I do. [*Monkey shakes its head in an affirmative manner.*] I'll remind you. A yellow banana.

MONKEY.

[*It nods yes and sticks its head into the bag or lunch kit. This time a yellow lemon is retrieved in the monkey's mouth.*]

YOU.

That's a yellow lemon. What happened this time?

MONKEY.

[*It whispers in your ear.*]

YOU.

You made a mistake! Why, I never make mistakes. [*Set the lemon aside and look back at the monkey. The monkey is nodding its head in an affirmative manner.*] Yes, I make mistakes every day. Are you sure you have a yellow banana?

MONKEY.

[*It nods affirmatively, reaches into the lunch bag or lunch kit, and brings out a yellow banana in its mouth.*]

YOU.

What do you do with a yellow banana?

MONKEY.

[*It whispers in your ear and nods to audience.*]

YOU.

Eat it? You got it! [*Stick the end of the banana in the monkey's mouth and look at your watch.*] You haven't got time to eat bananas. [*Pull the banana out of the monkey's mouth. Then manipulate the monkey's mouth into different pouting positions.*] Right after the show we will have time to eat.

MONKEY.

[*It nods its head affirmatively.*]

YOU.

[*Put the plastic fruit back into the lunch bag or lunch box.*] I could help you eat lunch. I like bananas, apples, and grapes. Are you going to eat this lemon? [*Monkey nods affirmatively.*] I'm not going to eat lunch with you.

April Rabbits

SUBJECT: Sharing / Rabbits / Spring

BOOKS TO READ:

Max and Ruby's First Greek Myth by Rosemary Wells (Dial Books for Young Readers, 1993).

Zomo the Rabbit told and illustrated by Gerald McDermott (Harcourt Brace Jovanovich, 1992).

It's Mine by Leo Lionni (Alfred A. Knopf, 1985).

MATERIALS: Finger puppets (one for each child): rabbits (pink, white, lavender, and purple felt; wiggly eyes; pompoms); hot glue gun and glue sticks; stuffed hippopotamus; book: *April Rabbits* by David Cleveland

SETUP: Make several rabbits of each color. Add wiggly eyes and pompom tails using hot glue.

As an alternative to felt finger puppets, children may make their own stick puppets out of paper, using their own designs or a preprinted design. Attach the paper puppets to craft sticks with hot glue.

Hand out the rabbit finger puppets. Instruct the children to make the motions suggested in the story with their puppets as you read the story.

THE SHOW

Read aloud *April Rabbits*, keeping the children actively involved in pantomiming the action. (On the 30th day of April, Robert does not see any rabbits. However, a hippopotamus enters the story. Keep the hippopotamus puppet hidden from the audience's view until this time. Slide it on your hand and bring it out after you read the line stating that a hippopotamus followed Robert home.)

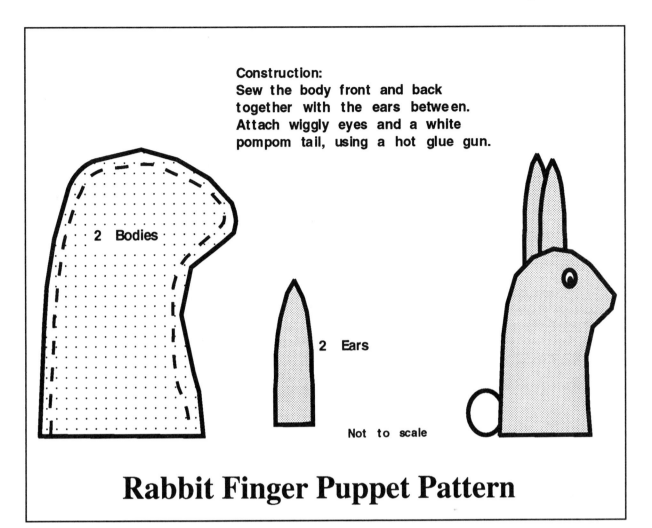

Construction:
Sew the body front and back together with the ears between. Attach wiggly eyes and a white pompom tail, using a hot glue gun.

2 Bodies

2 Ears

Not to scale

Rabbit Finger Puppet Pattern

Are You My Mother?

SUBJECT: Birds / Mothers / Babies

BOOKS TO READ:
> *A Mother for Choco* by Keiko Kasza (G. P. Putnam's Sons, 1992).
> *Where's Our Mama?* by Diane Goode (Dutton Children's Books, 1991).
> *Mama's Secret* by Maria Polushkin (Four Winds Press, 1984).

MATERIALS: Finger puppet: yellow baby bird; hand puppets: mother bird, cow, dog, kitten, hen; props: basket or bird nest, a white plastic egg (pantyhose container), toys—boat, plane, car, bulldozer. (No stage is required.)

SETUP: Lend the cow, dog, hen, and kitten hand puppets and the toy boat, plane, and car to children in the audience. Instruct them to make the sound of that animal or vehicle whenever the baby bird asks them if they are its mother. Put the toy bulldozer on a table nearby. Put the mother bird hand puppet on your right hand. Put the baby bird finger puppet inside the egg. Hold the basket or nest (with the white plastic egg in it) in your left hand. Start the show with the mother bird sitting on the nest.

THE SHOW

MOTHER BIRD.

My baby will be here soon, and I know it will be hungry. I must get something for my baby bird to eat. I'll be back. [*She leaves the nest. Fly her around behind you and drop her off your hand behind a book or something that gets her out of sight. Now the egg hatches. Open the egg and take the baby bird out and place it on your forefinger. Make motions to indicate that the baby bird is looking for its mother.*]

BABY BIRD.

Where is my mother? [*Baby bird looks around.*] I will go to look for her. [*Set the bird nest down. Walk the baby bird to each animal and toy vehicle in turn (in this order: kitten, hen, dog, cow, boat, plane, car, bulldozer), and ask (in the baby bird's voice), "Are you my mother?" The children should respond with the sound that the animal or vehicle makes, rather than with the answer "No."*]

BABY BIRD.

[*Baby bird approaches the bulldozer (on a table).*] "Mother, mother! Here I am mother!"

[*Drop the bird into the bulldozer's shovel.*] Oh, you are not my mother. You are a Snort. I have to get out of here! [*Pick up the bulldozer, and tip over the shovel with the bird in it, dropping the bird into the nest.*]

[*Slip the mother bird puppet onto your hand. On your other hand, slip the baby bird finger puppet onto one finger and hold the basket or bird nest with the rest of your hand. The baby bird should be on your forefinger and appear to be in the nest.*]

MOTHER BIRD.

Do you know who I am?

BABY BIRD.

Yes, I know who you are. You are not a kitten, not a hen, not a dog, and not a cow. You are not a boat, not a plane, not a car, and not a Snort! You are a bird, and you are my mother!

MOTHER.

That's my baby!

Based on the book *Are You My Mother?* by P. D. Eastman (Random House, 1960). Copyright © 1960 P. D. Eastman. Used with permission. Skits based on this book may not be performed professionally without the written consent of Random House.

Claude the Dog

SUBJECT: Gifts / Christmas

BOOKS TO READ:
>*Too Many Tamales* by Gary Soto (G. P. Putnam's Sons, 1993).
>Selections from *The Family Read-aloud Christmas Treasury* (Joy Street Books, 1989).

MATERIALS: Hand puppet: boy with hands that can pick up objects, "well-groomed" dog; "scruffy-looking" dog; props: tiny blanket and pillow, toy mouse; hand puppet stage.

SETUP: Place the boy puppet on your right hand and the well-groomed dog, Claude, on your left hand (Claude remains onstage during the entire skit).

THE SHOW

BOY.
Merry Christmas, Claude. We didn't forget you. See! Here's a dog pillow from Momma. [*Boy exits the stage and comes back with a miniature pillow, which he places on the playboard.*] A dog blanket from Poppa. [*Boy exits the stage and comes back with a miniature blanket, which he places on the playboard, next to the pillow.*] And a toy mouse from me. [*Boy exits the stage and comes back with a toy mouse, which he places on the playboard, next to the other items.*] That's all. Be a good dog, Claude. [*Boy exits the stage. Claude remains onstage. Take the boy puppet off your hand and put on the scruffy looking dog puppet.*]

BUMMER.
[*Bummer enters.*]

CLAUDE.
Look at all my presents, Bummer.

BUMMER.
My! You are a lucky dog, Claude.

CLAUDE.
Do you see my soft pillow, Bummer?

BUMMER.
I've never seen a pillow before, Claude. I sleep on the hard ground.

CLAUDE.
Here, you take my pillow, Bummer. [*Claude pushes the pillow toward Bummer.*]

BUMMER.
Oh, thank you, Claude.

CLAUDE.
Do you see my nice, warm blanket, Bummer?

BUMMER.
I've never seen a blanket, Claude. My nights are very cold.

CLAUDE.
Then you take my blanket, Bummer. [*Claude picks up the blanket and drapes it over Bummer.*]

BUMMER.
Thank you, Claude.

CLAUDE.
Do you see my toy? It's a mouse, Bummer.

BUMMER.
I've never had a toy, Claude. Sometimes I get very lonely.

CLAUDE.
Then take my toy mouse to keep you company, Bummer. [*Claude pushes the toy mouse toward Bummer.*]

BUMMER.
But you have no presents left, Claude.

CLAUDE.
My best present is at home, Bummer.

BUMMER.
You've made me so happy, Claude. I wish you a very merry Christmas.

CLAUDE.
Merry Christmas to you too, Bummer.

BUMMER.
[*Picks up the pillow in his paws and carries it offstage, returning to get the blanket, then the mouse. Take the Bummer puppet off your hand and put on the boy puppet while Claude remains onstage, barking.*]

BOY.
[*Boy enters.*] What's the matter, Claude?

CLAUDE.
[*Claude runs over to the boy and kisses him, loudly.*]

BOY.
We love you, Claude. [*Claude and the boy exit.*]

Don't Bother Me

SUBJECT: Monsters / Books

BOOKS TO READ:
Go West, Swamp Monsters by Mary B. Christian (Dial Press, 1985).
Arthur Babysits by Marc Brown (Little, Brown, 1992).
Bookstore Cat by Cindy Wheeler (Random House, 1994).

MATERIALS: Rod puppets: girl, stretch-neck monster (six-inch-diameter Styrofoam ball, felt, two large wiggly eyes, fake fur, three-foot-long dowel, colorful cloth, needle, thread); hot glue gun and glue sticks; thin metal rod or coat hanger; short dowel; broom holder; hand puppet stage. A sock puppet could also be used for the monster.

SETUP: Place the girl rod puppet on the playboard at stage left. Attach the metal rod or coat hanger to the puppet's right arm (used as a control stick). Attach the broom holder to the side of the playboard (facing you) at stage left. Attach the short dowel to the puppet's back and push the dowel into the broom holder. The puppet should be "sitting" on the playboard.

To make the stretch-neck monster puppet, hot-glue felt to the Styrofoam ball (cover the entire ball). Add large wiggly eyes, a pointed felt nose, and "sharp" felt teeth. Add fake fur for hair. Insert the dowel into the head as the puppet's neck, securing it with hot glue. Sew a colorful cloth cover for the three-foot-long dowel, leaving both ends of the cover open (it should fit loosely over the dowel). Slide the cover onto the dowel and secure the upper end to the head with hot glue. Using more of the fake fur, sew a "glove" resembling a large foot. Add black felt claws to the fingers ("toes") of the glove. Sew the glove to the bottom of the material covering the dowel, so that the dowel is located between the thumb and forefinger of the glove. (See art on page 14.)

Slip your right hand into the monster's foot. Grasp the dowel, drawing it downward while pushing the foot up close to the puppet's head. Stand in the puppet stage with the monster in your right hand, out of view of the audience, and the girl to your left.

THE SHOW

YOU.
Once upon a time, a little boy and a little girl went to the library. The boy teased the little girl.

YOU, IN BOY'S VOICE.
Victoria, a monster is coming.

GIRL.
Don't bother me, I'm looking for books. [*When the girl speaks, move the rod on which the arm is attached, as if to wave the boy away.*]

YOU, IN BOY'S VOICE.
A monster is coming! A monster is coming! I can see its eyes. [*Push the monster's head up so the audience can see its eyes.*]

GIRL.
Don't bother me, I'm looking for books. [*Puppeteer moves girl's arm again with the control stick.*]

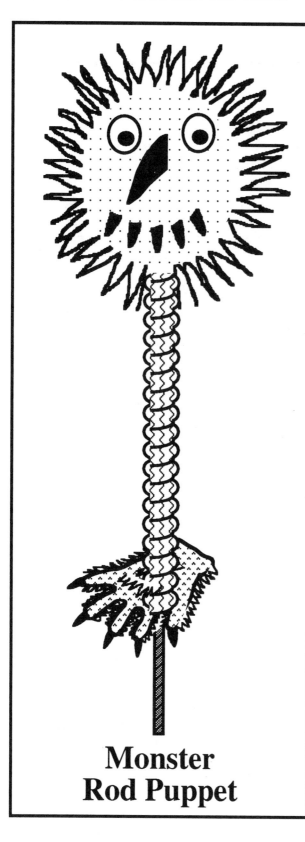

Monster Rod Puppet

YOU, IN BOY'S VOICE.
A monster is coming! A monster is coming!

GIRL.
Don't bother me, I'm looking for books. [*When the girl speaks, move the rod on which the arm is attached, as if to wave the boy away.*]

YOU.
[*Repeat these actions three more times, moving the monster closer to the girl each time, and raising it to reveal the nose, teeth, and feet in turn. Then, with the monster right next to the girl and your left hand on the end of the three-foot rod, say the following in the boy's voice:*] A monster is coming! A monster is coming! He's here! [*As you loudly say, "He's here!" shove the rod up into the loose material of the puppet's neck, aiming the head at the audience. Through the scrim you should see the audience jump with surprise. Pull the stick back down again. Your right hand is still in the monster's foot, which continues to rest upon the playboard. Push the rod up again, directing the puppet's head to the top of the stage. Turn the puppet's head around, so he appears to be looking backstage. Turn the puppet's head around again to face the audience and pull the rod down. Push the head toward the audience one more time. Pull it back.*]

YOU, IN BOY'S VOICE.
A monster is coming! A monster is coming!

GIRL.
Don't bother me, I'm—

YOU.
[*Make a loud growling or snorting sound as the monster. Pass the monster's head in front of the girl, and pull the girl offstage by pulling the rod out of the broom holder catch. Take the monster offstage with the girl.*]

The 4th of July Guy

SUBJECT: 4th of July / Clothes / Color

BOOKS TO READ:
A Color of His Own by Leo Lionni (Pantheon Books, c1975).
The Principal's New Clothes by Stephanie Calmenson (Scholastic, c1989).

MATERIALS: Large hand puppet: animal or person (I use a lion); props: blue shirt, red cap, pair of white cloth underpants or a pair of white plastic underpants (the kind that go over a diaper), large paper bag.

SETUP: Hold the puppet like a ventriloquist dummy. Place the clothes into the paper bag and have the bag next to you during the show.

THE SHOW

YOU.
Hey, Guy! Are you ready for the 4th of July?

GUY.
I'm not ready yet.

YOU.
Why not?

GUY.
I want to wear red, white, and blue—to be in style.

YOU.
Oh, that sounds good. Let's get you ready.

GUY.
My clothes are right here in my suitcase.

YOU.
[*Pick up the paper bag full of clothes and set it back down.*] This is your suitcase? I'm not impressed.

GUY.
I wasn't trying to impress you. I was trying to carry my clothes.

YOU.
All right. What do you want to put on first?

GUY.
I want my blue shirt. That should look snappy.

YOU.
[*Reach into the bag, pull out the blue shirt, and put it on the puppet. Let the puppet "help" you by making him grab a part of the shirt in his mouth and pushing his arms through the jacket sleeves.*] Sappy? I thought that you wanted to look smart.

GUY.
I said *snappy*, not sappy.

YOU.
Say, that does look nice. I'm impressed.

GUY.
Now, find something red.

YOU.
[*Reach into the bag, pull out the red cap, and put it on the puppet.*] That looks good. You need a new suitcase. If I carried my clothes in a paper bag, people would think that I was a bum.

GUY.
Don't worry about what other people think. What matters is what you think about yourself. I think that I want to put on something white.

YOU.
Okay. [*Reach into the paper bag, pull out the white underpants, and put them on the puppet.*] Now you are all dressed up in red, white, and blue.

GUY.

[*Guy looks down at his underpants.*] Hey, my underwear is hanging out. I can't go out and watch the parade with my underpants hanging out. I look ridiculous. People will think that I'm crazy.

YOU.

You just told me that it doesn't matter what other people think. It only matters what you think about yourself.

GUY.

Okay. I'm embarrassed. I think that I look terrible. I think that I'm not going to go anywhere if my underpants are hanging out.

YOU.

Maybe there is something else in your suitcase. [*Look into the bag.*] No, there isn't anything else in here. Why didn't you bring more pairs of pants?

GUY.

Because I was so excited about going to the parade. I was thinking about the parade and not about what I was putting into my suitcase. Maybe somebody here will give me their pants. [*Puppet looks out into the audience.*] Hey, you. Won't you let me borrow your pants?

YOU.

You can't borrow someone's pants right off their body. Then their underpants would be hanging out.

GUY.

Oh yeah! I didn't think about that.

YOU.

So what are you going to do about this "pants" problem?

GUY.

Can you take me shopping for a pair of pants?

YOU.

Yes. That's a good idea. Now, how are we going to get out of here and into a store if your underpants are hanging out?

GUY.

Put me inside the bag. I'll ride in the bag—no one will see me.

YOU.

[*Set the puppet down in the bag, with his head sticking out.*] Hey, Guy. What is your message for the 4th of July?

GUY.

There'll be sky-high fireworks this 4th of July. Wear red, white, and blue. I'll be looking for you. If you forget your pants and your spirits sag, just grab a sack—yes, wear that bag!

Jake the Cowboy

SUBJECT: Cowboys / Rodeos

BOOKS TO READ:
  Cowboy Rodeo by James Rice (Pelican, 1992).
  Matthew the Cowboy by Ruth Hooker (Albert Whitman, 1990).
  The Cowboy and the Black-Eyed Pea by Tony Johnston (G. P. Putnam's Sons, 1992).

MATERIALS: Ventriloquist dummy: Jake (wearing western clothes).

SETUP: Obtain a ventriloquist dummy (for suggestions on how to operate a ventriloquist dummy, see "Ventriloquism," p. xiii). Stand and face the audience, with the ventriloquist dummy on your hand. Use your free hand as a "chair" for the dummy.

THE SHOW

YOU.
  Hi Jake, I understand you live on a ranch.

JAKE.
  That's right.

YOU.
  What kind of ranch is it?

JAKE.
  What kinds are there?

YOU.
  Well, let's see. There's a chicken ranch.

JAKE.
  What does a chicken look like?

YOU.
  A chicken has feathers.

JAKE.
  That's not it.

YOU.
  Is it a sheep ranch?

JAKE.
  What does a sheep look like?

YOU.
  A sheep is kind of woolly.

JAKE.
  That's not it either.

YOU.
  How about a cattle ranch with cows?

JAKE.
  What does a cow look like?

YOU.
  Ooh, I know. A cow has horns.

JAKE.
  That's it. Toot, Toot!

YOU.
  Do you have a horse?

JAKE.
  What's that?

YOU.
  It's something you ride around on.

JAKE.
  Oh yeah! Rrrrooommm. Rrrooommm.

YOU.
  What is your horse's name?

JAKE.
  His name is Cow.

YOU.
  No, what's your horse's name?

JAKE.
  His name is Cow.

YOU.
Okay, okay! I suppose you feed him a lot of grass.

JAKE.
Oh yeah! Give him the gas. Give him the gas. Rrrooommm. Rrrooommm.

YOU.
Where is your ranch?

JAKE.
What do you mean "Where is it?"

YOU.
I mean what street is it on?

JAKE.
I don't know.

YOU.
You don't know what street you live on? These boys and girls know what street they live on.

JAKE.
They do?

YOU.
I know. What is the name of your ranch?

JAKE.
That's easy. The Rancho Viejo Apartments.

YOU.
The Rancho Viejo Apartments. Say, this horse you have named Cow—

JAKE.
Yeah?

YOU.
How many legs does he have?

JAKE.
No legs.

YOU.
No legs! How does he get around?

JAKE.
Two wheels.

YOU.
Two wheels. Sounds like a motorcycle to me.

JAKE.
That's what it is! Rrrooommm.

YOU.
Oh, please. Do you have any plans for the future?

JAKE.
What's that?

YOU.
I mean, are you looking forward to something? Most people are looking forward to something.

JAKE.
Oh, yeah. I'm going to be an astronaut.

YOU.
Now, how can a cowboy be an astronaut?

JAKE.
It's easy. I've got a lot of space in my head. [*Figure raises and lowers his eyebrows.*]

YOU.
What are you looking at?

JAKE.
Girls.

YOU.
Are there some cute girls here?

JAKE.
Yeah!

YOU.
Would you like to take one of these girls out on a date?

JAKE.
Yeah!

YOU.
Everyone in this room will go out on a date sometime.

JAKE.
Me, too.

YOU.
Including you. If you took one of these girls out on a date, and she said she was feeling kind of empty, where would you take her?

JAKE.
To the gas station for a fill-up.

YOU.
Do you have any money?

JAKE.
A pocketful.

YOU.
How much is a pocketful of money?

JAKE.
Thirty-nine cents.

YOU.
Can you read?

JAKE.
No. I just watch girls.

YOU.
Do you want to learn to read?

JAKE.
Not me.

YOU.
If you don't learn to read, you'll be a dummy all your life.

JAKE.
That's me.

YOU.
Say good-bye, Jake.

JAKE.
Bye girls! [*He waves at the audience.*]

The Library Is Closed

SUBJECT: Libraries / Reading

BOOKS TO READ:
 How My Library Grew, by Dinah by Martha Alexander (H. W. Wilson, 1983).
 The Wednesday Surprise by Eve Bunting (Clarion Books, 1989).
 Check It Out! by Gail Gibbons (Harcourt Brace Jovanovich, 1985).

MATERIALS: Hand puppets: two mice, librarian; cardboard or poster board car silhouette with a window cut out; a black light; fluorescent spray paint; hand puppet stage.

SETUP: Spray paint the librarian puppet's clothing and hair, the mice puppets, and the car silhouette. Attach the black light to the playboard. The play is performed in black light because mice are nocturnal animals. The setting is nighttime in the library. The lights are off and the mice are roaming around. Turn on the black light to illuminate the puppets and car.

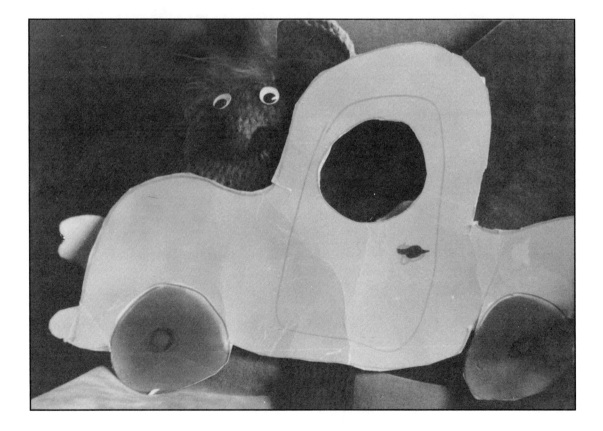

THE SHOW

MORSELS.
[*Morsels enters at stage left.*] I'm ready to check out some books. I need something to read. Let me at them.

LIBRARIAN.
[*Librarian enters at stage right.*] The library is closed. You can't check out any books. Get out of here.

MORSELS.
I need something to read. Why is the library closed?

LIBRARIAN.
School will be out for the summer. We're taking inventory in here. We need to count all the books. We need to see what's missing.

MORSELS.
What am I supposed to do? I need something to read. You can't just close the library. What am I going to do?

LIBRARIAN.
You can go to the public library. They have plenty of books there, and they're open all year. I'm sure you can find something good to read there.

MORSELS.
Where's the public library, and how do I get there?

LIBRARIAN.
The library is three miles from here. You need a car to get there. Now don't hang around here, or you could become cat food. [*Librarian exits at stage right.*]

MORSELS.
I'll have to go outside, and see if I can find a car.

GROUND.
[*Ground enters at stage right.*] Hey, got any new books? I need something to read. Where are the new books in the library?

MORSELS.
The library's closed. You can't check out any books.

GROUND.
Why is the library closed? I need something to read.

MORSELS.
They're taking inventory because school is closing. The librarian said we have to go to the public library to get books. She said not to hang around here because we might become cat food. I wonder what that means.

GROUND.
I wonder what makes the librarian so crabby!

MORSELS.
It's probably because we ask her stupid questions all day.

GROUND.
She got angry with me because I lost a library book.

MORSELS.
Did you ever find it?

GROUND.
Yes, I found it.

MORSELS.
Where did you find it?

GROUND.
In the refrigerator.

MORSELS.
What was your library book doing in the refrigerator?

GROUND.
Dancing with the leftovers?

[*Meow loudly and bring your hands together so the two mice are hugging each other.*]

MORSELS.
What was that?

GROUND.
It sounded like a cat.

[*Separate the two mice.*]

MORSELS.

My name is Morsels. What's your name?

GROUND.

My name is Ground.

[*Meow loudly and put your hands together so the two mice are hugging each other again.*]

MORSELS.

There's a cat in here. We better leave before we become cat food.

GROUND.

How are we going to get to the public library?

MORSELS.

We need a car.

GROUND.

I'll go outside and see if I can find one. [*Ground exits at stage right and returns with a car. Pick up the car by the rod. A window should be cut in the car, so the mouse can be seen through the window.*]

GROUND.

Come on, Morsels. We are on our way to the public library. I bet they have some new books there. We'll be looking for you at the public library, too. Bye-bye.

[*The two mice and the car exit at stage left.*]

Mother, Mother, I Want Another

SUBJECT: Love / Mothers / Family Life

BOOKS TO READ:
> *Hazel's Amazing Mother* by Rosemary Wells (Dial Books for Young Readers, 1985).
> *Trade-in Mother* by Marisabina Russo (Greenwillow Books, 1993).
> *Is Your Mama a Llama?* by Deborah Guarino (Scholastic, 1989).

MATERIALS: Hand puppets: mouse (two puppets), duck, frog, pig, donkey; prop: small bed that fits on the playboard; hand puppet stage.

SETUP: Place the bed on the playboard at stage right and the baby mouse puppet (with your right hand inside the puppet) in the bed. Put the mother mouse puppet on your left hand.

THE SHOW

MOTHER MOUSE.
> [*Mother Mouse enters at stage left.*] Time for bed. Good night. [*She tucks the baby mouse into bed.*] Now, dear, we've brushed your teeth, and I've read you a bedtime story. It's time for you to go to sleep. [*She leans down and kisses the baby mouse, making a loud kissing sound. She starts to leave.*] [*The baby mouse suddenly sits up.*]

BABY MOUSE.
> [*Baby Mouse sits up, suddenly.*] Mother, Mother, I want another.

MOTHER MOUSE.
> [*She talks to herself as she exits.*] Another! My baby mouse wants another mother! Where will I find another mother for my baby? [*Take off the mother mouse puppet and put on the duck puppet. Mother mouse (offstage) says, "Please Mrs. Duck, come to our house and help put my baby mouse to bed. Tonight he wants another mother."*]

MRS. DUCK.
> [*Mrs. Duck enters at stage left and walks over to the baby mouse.*] Quack, quack, mousie, don't you fret. I'll bring you worms both fat and wet.

BABY MOUSE.
> Mother, Mother, I want another.

MRS. DUCK.
> [*Mrs. Duck exits at stage left. Take off the duck puppet and put on the frog puppet.*]

MOTHER MOUSE.
> [*Offstage:*] Please, Mrs. Frog, come to our house and help put my baby mouse to bed. Tonight he wants another mother.

MRS. FROG.
> [*Mrs. Frog enters at stage left and walks over to the baby mouse.*] Croak, croak, mousie, close your eyes. I will bring you big fat flies.

BABY MOUSE.
> Mother, Mother, I want another.

MRS. FROG.

[*Mrs. Frog exits at stage left. Take off the frog puppet and put on the pig puppet.*]

MOTHER MOUSE.

[*Offstage:*] Please, Mrs. Pig, come to our house and help put my baby mouse to bed. Tonight he wants another mother.

MRS. PIG.

[*Mrs. Pig enters at stage left and walks over to the baby mouse.*] Oink, oink, mousie, go to sleep. I'll bring some carrots for you to keep.

BABY MOUSE.

Mother, Mother, I want another.

MRS. PIG.

[*Mrs. Pig exits at stage left. Take off the pig puppet and put on the donkey puppet.*]

MOTHER MOUSE.

[*Offstage:*] Please, Mrs. Donkey, come to our house and help put my baby mouse to bed. Tonight he wants another mother.

MRS. DONKEY.

[*Mrs. Donkey enters at stage left and walks over to the baby mouse.*] Hee-haw, mousie, hush-a-bye. I'll sing you a lullaby.

BABY MOUSE.

No more mothers! I want another *kiss*!

MRS. DONKEY.

[*Mrs. Donkey leans down and kisses the baby mouse, making a loud kissing sound, and exits at stage left.*]

[*Bring out each puppet in turn to lean down and kiss the baby mouse, making a loud kissing sound—the duck, the frog, and the pig. Put on the mother mouse puppet.*]

MOTHER MOUSE.

[*Mother Mouse enters at stage left and walks over to the baby mouse. She leans down and kisses the baby mouse, making a loud kissing sound. She turns to leave.*]

BABY MOUSE.

Mother, Mother, I want another.

MOTHER MOUSE.

Of course. [*She leans over and gives the baby mouse another kiss, making a loud kissing sound.*]

Mrs. Beaver's Thanksgiving

SUBJECT: Thanksgiving

BOOKS TO READ:
Thanksgiving Treat by Catherine Stock (Bradbury Press, 1990).
Daisy's Crazy Thanksgiving by Margery Cuyler (Henry Holt, 1990).
'Twas the Night Before Thanksgiving by Dav Pilkey (Orchard Books, 1990).

MATERIALS: Hand puppet: a beaver; props: large paper sack, brown feathers, plastic food (vegetables and dessert—e.g., green beans, ear of corn, bread, candy, cookie, donut, ice cream bar, green sucker).

SETUP: Cut a hole in the back of the sack for your hand (the hole should be cut toward the bottom of the sack; see the photo below). Cut a larger hole in the front of the sack to create a "stage" for the puppet (the hole should be cut toward the bottom of the sack).

Put the feathers into the sack. Place the puppet at the center of the sack. Place the plastic food inside the sack (the vegetables toward one side and the cookies and candy toward the other side). Sit in a chair, facing the audience, with the sack resting in your lap.

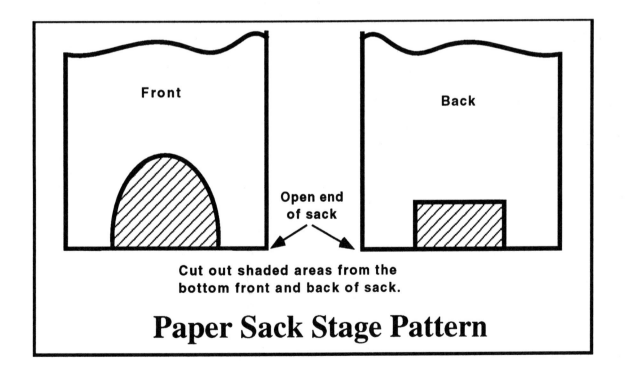

Front

Back

Open end of sack

Cut out shaded areas from the bottom front and back of sack.

Paper Sack Stage Pattern

THE SHOW

YOU.
Hello, Mrs. Beaver. Are you fixing Thanksgiving dinner?

PUPPET.
Yes, I am.

YOU.
What are you having?

PUPPET.
Oh, the usual.

YOU.
And what is that?

PUPPET.
Cookies. [*Puppet pulls out a cookie, which you hold up.*]

YOU.
What else?

PUPPET.
[*Puppet pulls out a donut, which you hold up.*]

YOU.
Anything else?

PUPPET.
[*Puppet pulls out an ice cream bar, which you hold up.*]

YOU.
This is not a good dinner.

PUPPET.
What's wrong with it?

YOU.
You need something green.

PUPPET.
You should have said that in the first place. [*Puppet pulls out a green sucker.*]

YOU.
I mean a green vegetable.

PUPPET.
How is this? [*Puppet pulls out green beans.*]

YOU.
Yes, that's what I mean. Do you have any other vegetables?

PUPPET.
[*Puppet pulls out an ear of corn.*]

YOU.
This is much better, but there is something missing for Thanksgiving dinner. Boys and girls, do you know what's missing from this dinner?

CHILDREN.
Turkey!

PUPPET.
[*Puppet rattles around in the sack as if it were chasing a turkey.*] I can't catch him. [*Puppet rattles around in the sack again.*] Whew! He sure can run fast. [*Make the feathers fall out of the sack as the puppet "chases" the turkey inside the sack.*]

YOU.
Go ahead and cook these vegetables. I'm sure you can catch that turkey.

PUPPET.
Thanks. I'll get him. [*Puppet continues to chase after the turkey.*]

YOU.
[*Quickly place the sack out of sight, as the children will want to see the "turkey."*]

Poppy the Panda

SUBJECT: Clothes / Pandas

BOOKS TO READ:
Peter's Pockets by Eve Rice (Greenwillow Books, 1989).
Jesse Bear, What Will You Wear? by Nancy White Carlstrom (Macmillan, 1986).
Milton the Early Riser by Robert Krauss (Simon & Schuster, 1972).

MATERIALS: Hand puppet: panda bear; props: doll dress, roller-skates, umbrella, shoe, sneaker, fruit bowl, towel, shower cap, roll of toilet tissue, hair ribbon that can be tied in a bow around the panda bear's neck.

SETUP: Hand out the props to the children in class (the shoe and the sneaker should be given to the same child). Lend the Poppy the Panda bear puppet to a girl in the class. She will be walking through the audience, trying to find something suitable for Poppy to wear. She will be assisted by you, "acting" as the mother of Katie. You should speak for both Poppy and Katie.

THE SHOW

KATIE.
It's time for bed!

POPPY.
I can't sleep when I'm unhappy.

KATIE.
I didn't know that you were unhappy.

POPPY.
Well, I am! Everyone has something nice to wear but me. Your doll has a fancy dress. And your soldier has a fine suit and hat. Why, even your cat has a collar. But what do I have to wear? Nothing at all!

KATIE.
I'll have to do something about that.

POPPY.
Good. Otherwise, I doubt if I'll ever want to go to bed.

GIRL PLAYING KATIE.
[*She takes Poppy to the child who has the doll dress and tells the child to try the dress on Poppy.*]

KATIE.
There! That looks good on you. Now will you come to bed?

POPPY.
I hate it! I am a boy Panda and I will not wear a dress.

KATIE.
Fussy, fussy, fussy.

GIRL PLAYING KATIE.
[*She takes Poppy to the child who has the roller skates and tells the child to put the skates on Poppy. Then the child gives Poppy a push and lets him roll until he falls over.*]

KATIE.
Are you hurt? I'm so sorry. Cheer up, Poppy. We'll find something else for you to wear.

POPPY.
Something without wheels, please.

GIRL PLAYING KATIE.

[*She takes Poppy to the child who has the umbrella and tells the child to give the umbrella to Poppy.*]

POPPY.

Nobody wears an umbrella!

GIRL PLAYING KATIE.

[*She takes Poppy to the child who has the shoe and the sneaker and tells the child to put them on Poppy.*]

POPPY.

These won't do. They don't even match.

KATIE.

You're so hard to please, Poppy!

GIRL PLAYING KATIE.

[*She takes Poppy to the child who has the fruit bowl and tells the child to put the fruit bowl on Poppy's head.*]

POPPY.

I am your best friend, not a banana.

GIRL PLAYING KATIE.

[*She takes Poppy to the child who has the towel and tells the child to wrap the towel around Poppy.*]

POPPY.

[*He shakes his head no.*]

GIRL PLAYING KATIE.

[*She takes Poppy to the child who has the shower cap and tells the child to put the shower cap on Poppy's head.*]

POPPY.

[*Poppy shakes his head no.*]

GIRL PLAYING KATIE.

[*She takes Poppy to the child who has the roll of toilet tissue and tells the child to wrap the toilet tissue around Poppy.*]

POPPY.

Where do you get such ideas? You've made me look like a package.

KATIE.

What are we to do with you, you silly panda?

POPPY.

Just find me something to wear, something sensible. Is that so difficult?

GIRL PLAYING KATIE.

[*She takes Poppy to the child who has the hair ribbon and tells the child to tie the ribbon in a bow around Poppy's neck.*]

KATIE.

Now, how's that?

POPPY.

I love my ribbon.

KATIE.

Now we are ready for bed.

POPPY.

I can't wait to show off my ribbon.

KATIE.

Tomorrow. But now, good night.

POPPY.

Good night.

The Principal

SUBJECT: School / Principals / Students

BOOKS TO READ:
  Miss Nelson Is Missing! by Harry Allard (Houghton Mifflin, 1977).
  Move Over, Twerp by Martha Alexander (Dial Press, 1981).

MATERIALS: A black robe, a principal mask (see below), five different hats (one for each "student" character): knit cap, cowboy hat, baseball cap, girl's bonnet with a ribbon, beret; a table.

SETUP: Put on the black robe. Place the table in an area that will be behind you as you face the audience. Place the five hats on the table.

Principal mask available from Grey Seal Puppets, 225 West Fourth Street, Charlotte, NC 28202; call (704) 374-0346.

THE SHOW

Hold the principal mask in front of your face (using the rod) while you are reciting the principal's lines. Put on a hat while you are reciting the lines of the students.

THE PRINCIPAL.
Send in student #1. He says reading is no fun.

[*Turn around so that you have your back to the audience. Place the mask on the table. Put on the knit cap. Change your face by curling your upper lip under itself, holding it tight against your upper gums, so that your upper teeth are showing (see picture). Turn around to face the audience. Ask your audience to make the same face that you are making. Put your hands underneath your arms, with your thumbs sticking out, and have the audience do the same.*]

STUDENT #1.
It's books that I don't want to read
'Cause they're as boring as can be
My teacher told me to read some more
That's why I threw my book on the floor.

It's a terrible thing you make me do
Reading and sitting in school all day
I want to be free to run and play
So let me go home, what do you say?

[*Turn around so that you have your back to the audience. Place the hat on the table. Hold the mask in front of your face. Turn around to face the audience.*]

THE PRINCIPAL.
Reading gives you wings
Changes the way you look at things.
Go back and give it another try
We want you to read, and read, and fly!

Send in student #2. I wonder what he doesn't want to do?

[*Turn around so that you have your back to the audience. Place the mask on the table. Put on the cowboy hat. Change your face contorting your mouth to one side (see picture). Turn around to face the audience. Ask your audience to make the same face that you are making.*]

STUDENT #2.
[*Speak with a cowboy drawl*]

It's this math that I can't abide
Add, subtract, multiply and divide
I don't want to do any more
So I slid from my chair to the floor.

It's a terrible thing you make me do
Math and sitting in school all day
I want to be free to run and play
So let me go home, what do you say?

[*Turn around so that you have your back to the audience. Place the hat on the table. Hold the mask in front of your face. Turn around to face the audience.*]

THE PRINCIPAL.
Math is a tool! It's a subject you
    need to pass
Did you hear what I said?
Now go back to your class
To put tools in your head.

Send in student #3. He is another stubborn rascal I see.

[*Turn around so that you have your back to the audience. Place the mask on the table. Put on the baseball cap. Change your face by pushing your tongue down between your lower teeth and your lower lip (see picture). Turn around to face the audience. Ask your audience to make the same face that you are making.*]

STUDENT #3.
Teacher says that I must write
And write and write some more.
But the words won't come and my
    brain is numb
And that's why my paper I tore!

It's a terrible thing you make me do
Writing and sitting in school all day
I want to be free to run and play
So let me go home, what do you say?

[*Turn around so that you have your back to the audience. Place the hat on the table. Hold the mask in front of your face. Turn around to face the audience.*]

THE PRINCIPAL.
Writing opens doors
Writing says you are happy or sad or
    even that you care
Writing letters, writing books
Writing is your mouth when you
    can't be there!

Send in student #4. I know I've seen her before!

[*Turn around so that you have your back to the audience. Place the mask on the table. Put on the girl's bonnet. Change your face by pulling your upper lip down over your upper teeth, sticking out your lower lip in a pout, and "squinching" up your eyes (see picture). Turn around to face the audience. Ask your audience to make the same face that you are making. Twirl the ribbon on your hat.*]

STUDENT #4.

The teacher put me in a spelling bee
And spelling is really not for me.
I thought and figured and wanted to
    shout
I finally gave up and passed right out.

It's a terrible thing you make me do
Spelling and sitting in school all day
I want to be free to run and play
So let me go home, what do you say?

[*Turn around so that you have your
back to the audience. Place the hat on
the table. Hold the mask in front of
your face. Turn around to face the
audience.*]

THE PRINCIPAL.

Spelling is the key to reading and
    writing
Spelling words right is very exciting
Go back and try. You know the reason
    why
To help you read and write and fly!

Send in student #5. These students all
need some drive.

[*Turn around so that you have your
back to the audience. Place the mask on
the table. Put on the beret. Change your
face by pursing your lips together and
sticking them out as far as you can, and
by pulling on your ears (see picture).
Turn around to face the audience. Ask
your audience to make the same face
that you are making.*]

STUDENT #5.

There is just too much science
Growing plants, feeding ants
Volcanoes erupting, dirt eroded
I studied and studied and finally
    exploded.

It's a terrible thing you make me do
Science and sitting in school all day
I want to be free to run and play
So let me go home, what do you say?

[*Turn around so that you have your
back to the audience. Place the hat on
the table. Hold the mask in front of
your face. Turn around to face the
audience.*]

THE PRINCIPAL.

Pull your self together
For science is the clue
The mysteries of the universe
Will be revealed to you.

And now my students are all at work
    I see
Reading, writing, spelling, math and
    science, busy as can be.
Oh, what is this? Wings and doors,
    tools and clues, a key.
Ah, my students, some day you will
    fly, I see!

[*Take a bow and exit the stage.*]

Rita Readalot

SUBJECT: Libraries / Reading

BOOKS TO READ:

Beatrice Doesn't Want To by Laura Numeroff (Franklin Watts, 1981).
Too Many Books by Caroline F. Bauer (Viking, 1984).
Clara and the Bookwagon by Nancy Smiler Levinson (HarperTrophy, 1988).

MATERIALS: Large hand puppet: Rita Readalot; fluffy toilet-lid cover; yarn; Velcro; hot glue gun and glue sticks; hand puppet stage.

SETUP: Make three wigs for the puppet using yarn, Velcro, and hot glue (synthetic wigs may be used). Glue a piece of Velcro to the head of the puppet. Place one hand into the puppet's head and your other hand inside the puppet's hand.

THE SHOW

RITA.

[*Rita enters at center stage wearing first wig.*] My name is Rita Readalot. One day I went to the library to look around. The librarian said I needed to get the library habit. I told her I didn't want one. My mom says I already have too many bad habits. The librarian said this was a good habit. She told me to go to the library every week, check out some books, read them, and bring them back the next week and get some more.

That is what I have been doing. I'm having fun learning about places and people, and I've been reading so much that my eyeballs itch. [*Puppet scratches her eyes.*] In fact, my head itches. [*Puppet scratches her head, pulls off her yarn wig, drops it, and scratches her head.*]

Whoops! What did I do that for? Just a minute. [*Puppet leaves stage area, puts on the second hair wig, and reappears. She pats her wig, takes it off, looks at it, and throws it behind her.*]

That's not my hair. [*Puppet leaves stage, puts on the third wig, and reappears onstage. She pats her wig, takes it off, looks at it, and throws it behind her.*]

That's not it either! My room is a mess. I can't find anything! [*Puppet leaves stage area, puts on a fuzzy toilet lid cover, and reappears onstage.*]

This feels much better! [*Puppet pats her head, takes the toilet lid cover off, looks at it.*]

What is this thing? It's a toilet lid cover. Oh, no! [*Puppet throws it behind her, exits stage, puts on her original yarn wig, and reappears onstage.*]

I must clean my room soon. What do *you* need to do? Get the library habit. That's right. Check out some books, read them, and go back to the library for more. You will meet new people, go to new places, read some scary stories, and see some funny faces. Just make sure your funny face gets to a library!

Part II

Folktales, Fairytales, and Fables

Chicken Little

SUBJECT: Chickens / Foxes / Folktales

BOOKS TO READ:
Rosie's Walk by Pat Hutchins (Macmillan, 1968).
Flossy and the Fox by Patricia C. McKissack (Dial Books for Young Readers, 1986)

MATERIALS: Hand puppets: chicken, goose, duck, turkey, fox; props: tiny tree or artificial flowers, plastic ear of corn; mesh bag (e.g., grapefruit bag); hand puppet stage.

SETUP: Place the tree or artificial flowers on the playboard at stage left.

THE SHOW

CHICKEN LITTLE.
[Chicken Little enters at stage left.] What a beautiful day. The sun is shining, the birds are singing, and I . . . [Say "BONK!" while quickly lowering and raising Chicken Little's head. Chicken Little looks up at the sky.] Oh, the sky is falling! Oh, help, the sky is falling! I must go tell my friends.

DUCKY LUCKY.
[Ducky Lucky enters at stage right.] Hi there, Chicken Little.

CHICKEN LITTLE.
The sky is falling. The sky is falling. I just got bonked on the head.

DUCKY LUCKY.
[Ducky Lucky looks up at the sky.] It is? Maybe we better go tell our friends that the sky is falling. Does your head hurt?

CHICKEN LITTLE.
No. It was just a little piece of the sky that fell.

DUCKY LUCKY.
I'm going to tell my friends about this. I don't want to get bonked on the head. [Ducky Lucky exits at stage right.]

CHICKEN LITTLE.
It's almost time for lunch. I hope that I can find something good for lunch.

TURKEY LURKEY.
[Turkey Lurkey enters at stage right.] Oh hi, Chicken Little. What's up?

CHICKEN LITTLE.
The sky is falling. I just got bonked on the head. You better be careful.

TURKEY LURKEY.
Oh no. Oh no. The sky is falling. I better go tell my friends. I don't want to get bonked on the head. [Turkey Lurkey exits at stage right.]

CHICKEN LITTLE.
I haven't found anything to eat for lunch. [Chicken Little looks up at the sky.] I hope that I don't get bonked on the head again.

GOOSEY LOOSEY.
[Goosey Loosey enters at stage right.] How are you doing there, Chicken Little? Nice day, isn't it?

CHICKEN LITTLE.
The sky is falling. The sky is falling. I'm telling you—I just got bonked on the head.

GOOSEY LOOSEY.
Are you sure that the sky is falling? I've never heard of such a thing. Where did it hit you?

CHICKEN LITTLE.
It bonked me on the head. I'm telling you—the sky is really falling. It landed on my head.

GOOSEY LOOSEY.

I better go tell my friends that the sky is falling. I don't want anybody else to get bonked on the head. [*Goosey Loosey exits at stage right.*]

CHICKEN LITTLE.

Everybody is going to tell their friends about the sky falling. I better go tell my friends, too. Lunch will have to wait. [*Chicken Little exits at stage left.*]

FOXY LOXY.

[*Foxy Loxy enters at stage left carrying a mesh bag containing an ear of corn.*] Say, what a fine bunch of chicken dinners. I'm looking for lunch, too. All those birds would make a feast for me. They were looking for lunch. I know that they like corn. I'll bet that they would like to have the corn in this bag. [*Foxy Loxy places the bag on the playboard at stage right. Use your right hand to situate the bag on the playboard with the opening hanging over the back of the stage.*] I'm going to enjoy my chicken lunch. Come on, little birdies. It's time for lunch. [*Foxy Loxy exits at stage left.*]

CHICKEN LITTLE.

[*Chicken Little enters at stage left.*] Oh, I'm so hungry. I haven't found anything to eat . . . corn! I see corn! That will be my lunch. [*Grab the top of the mesh bag with your right hand and hold it open while you stuff Chicken Little into the bag. Remove your hand from the puppet, leaving Chicken Little in the bag.*] Oh, I have found my lunch at last.

DUCKY LUCKY.

[*Ducky Lucky enters at stage left.*] Chicken Little, have you found some corn? It looks like I have found my lunch. Move over. Let me have some! [*Stuff Ducky Lucky into the bag. Remove your hand from the puppet, leaving Ducky Lucky in the bag.*]

TURKEY LURKEY.

[*Turkey Lurkey enters at stage left.*] Is that corn I see there? It looks like I have found my lunch. Move over and make room for me! [*Stuff Turkey Lurkey into the bag. Remove your hand from the puppet, leaving Turkey Lurkey in the bag.*]

GOOSEY LOOSEY.

[*Goosey Loosey enters at stage left.*] Have you found something to eat for lunch? Let me have some. Move over! Let me have some corn. I'm hungry, too. [*Stuff Goosey Loosey into the bag. Remove your hand from the puppet, leaving Goosey Loosey in the bag. The bag should be resting on the playboard at stage right.*]

FOXY LOXY.

[*Foxy Loxy enters at stage left.*] Aha! My lunch has arrived. And what a tasty lunch it will be. Whom shall I eat first? Should it be the chicken or the turkey or the duck or the goose? [*He tries to pick up the bag.*] Oh, this bag is heavy. This bag is too heavy. Maybe if I take a nap I will be strong enough to carry it. Just a short nap should do it. [*Lay down Foxy Loxy on the playboard at stage left, next to the tree prop or artificial flowers.*]

GOOSEY LOOSEY.

[*Put your right hand into Goosey Loosey and pull her out of the bag.*] Oh, that was a dirty trick. I wonder who put the corn in that bag. [*She walks over to Foxy Loxy.*] Say, it was you! What a naughty thing to do. You are a bad fox. [*She pecks Foxy Loxy.*] Take that!

FOXY LOXY.

Ouch! The fleas are terrible this year. [*Foxy Loxy doesn't move.*]

[*Goosey Loosey at stage right. Drop the puppet off your hand.*]

TURKEY LURKEY.

[*Put your right hand into Turkey Lurkey and pull her out of the bag.*] I wonder who put the corn in that bag. What a dirty trick to trap us in a bag. [*She looks around.*] Foxy Loxy—it was you! What a naughty thing to do. You are a bad fox. [*She pecks Foxy Loxy.*] Take that!

FOXY LOXY.

Ouch! The fleas are terrible this year. [*Foxy Loxy doesn't move.*]

[*Turkey Lurkey exits at stage right. Drop the puppet off your hand.*]

DUCKY LUCKY.

[*Put your right hand into Ducky Lucky and pull him out of the bag.*] I wonder who put the corn into that bag. What a dirty trick to trap us in a bag. [*He looks around.*] Foxy Loxy—it was you! What a naughty thing to do. You are a bad fox. [*He pecks Foxy Loxy.*] Take that!

FOXY LOXY.

Ouch! The fleas are terrible this year. [*Foxy Loxy doesn't move.*]

[*Ducky Lucky exits at stage right. Drop the puppet off your hand.*]

CHICKEN LITTLE.

[*Put your right hand into Chicken Little and pull him out of the bag.*] I wonder who put the corn into that bag. What a dirty trick to trap us in a bag. [*He looks around.*] Foxy Loxy—it was you! What a naughty thing to do. You are a bad fox. [*He pecks Foxy Loxy.*] Take that! [*He exits at stage right.*]

FOXY LOXY.

[*Foxy Loxy gets up.*] Ouch! The fleas are terrible this year. [*He looks toward stage right.*] My chicken lunch is ready. [*He walks over to the empty bag.*] My chicken lunch is gone! What happened to my lunch? They must have left while I was sleeping. Well, that's what I get for taking a nap. The next time I catch them I'll eat them right on the spot. I hope that I can catch them again.

GOOSEY LOOSEY.

[*Goosey Loosey enters at stage right.*] There won't be a next time, Foxy Loxy. [*She chases Foxy Loxy toward stage left, pecking him all the way.*] Take that! Take that!

FOXY LOXY.

Help! Help! [*Foxy Loxy exits at stage left.*]

GOOSEY LOOSEY.

[*Goosey Loosey exits at stage left, still chasing Foxy Loxy.*] Take that!

Cinderella

SUBJECT: Fairytales

BOOKS TO READ:
    Tattercoats by Flora Annie Steel (Bradbury Press, 1976).
    Rapunzel, retold by Barbara Rogasky (Holiday House, 1982).
    Thorn Rose by the Brothers Grimm (Bradbury Press, 1975).

MATERIALS: Props: a real glass slipper (available at discount jewelry stores and general merchandise stores), cutout pictures—Cinderella in rags, baby boy, two stepsisters, stepmother, fairy godfather, fairy godmother, frogs, mice, pumpkin, Cinderella in a jogging suit, new car, golden coach, several horses, the prince with Cinderella (wearing a ballroom dress), hiking boot, the prince with Cinderella (wearing a glass slipper); a basket or box to hold these cutouts; flannel board; felt; white glue.

SETUP: Glue a piece of felt onto the back of each picture.

THE SHOW

YOU.

Once upon a time there was a girl named Cinderella, [*place Cinderella in rags on the flannel board*] who lived with her little brother [*place a picture of a baby boy on the board*]. She didn't have a little brother? [*Take him off the board.*] She had two stepsisters. [*Place them on the board.*] She also had a stepmother [*place her on the board*], who was always telling her what to do.

One day the prince announced that there would be a grand ball, where he would pick a bride from among the women attending. The stepsisters and stepmother got dressed and went to the ball. [*Take the stepsisters and stepmother off the board.*] Cinderella was left by herself. She started to cry because she wanted to go to the ball, too.

Then her fairy godfather came to see her. [*Place him on the board. Pause while the audience reacts.*]

She didn't have a fairy godfather? Oh, it was a fairy godmother. [*Replace the godfather with the godmother.*] Her fairy godmother asked her why she was crying. Cinderella told her she wanted

to go to the ball. Her fairy godmother asked her if she had any friends around the house. Cinderella told her that she had her friends the frogs, who stayed by the fireplace. [*Place the frogs on the flannel board. Pause while the audience reacts.*]

She didn't have frogs in the house? She had mice? [*Remove the frogs and replace them with mice.*] The fairy godmother asked her for a pumpkin. [*Place a pumpkin on the flannel board*]. She waved her magic wand, and changed the pumpkin into a new car. [*Remove the mice and pumpkin and put a new car on the flannel board. Pause while the audience reacts.*]

She didn't get a new car? She got a coach? Let's see. Oh, yes. Here is a coach. And what? Horses, yes, horses. She changed the mice into horses. [*Place the coach and horses on the flannel board. Take the car off the board.*]

Cinderella told the fairy godmother that she couldn't go to the ball because she didn't have anything nice to wear. The fairy godmother waved her magic wand and changed Cinderella's rags into a nice new jogging suit. [*Remove the Cinderella in rags and replace her with a Cinderella in a jogging suit. Pause while the audience reacts.*]

She didn't get a jogging suit? She got a dress? She had to wear a dress? [*Remove the Cinderella in a jogging suit and replace it with Cinderella and the prince in ballroom clothes.*] Yes, her rags were changed into a beautiful dress, and she was ready for the ball.

Before she left, her fairy godmother warned her that she must be home by midnight, because at the stroke of twelve everything would change back to what it had been.

Cinderella met the prince and they danced and danced, until the clock struck midnight. Suddenly, Cinderella remembered that she was supposed to

be home by midnight, before everything changed back to what it had been. She ran as fast as she could. On the way, she lost her hiking boot. [*Replace the Cinderella and prince in ballroom clothes with a hiking boot. Pause while the audience reacts.*]

She didn't wear hiking boots? She wore glass slippers? [*Replace the hiking boot with a picture of the prince and Cinderella with glass slippers.*] Yes, she lost her glass slipper, but the prince found it, and when he put it on her foot, it fit. Then she took the other glass slipper out of her pocket, and he knew that she was truly Cinderella.

This is the glass slipper that Cinderella had in her pocket. [*Hold up a real glass slipper for all to see.*] And they lived happily ever after.

The City Mouse and the Country Mouse

SUBJECT: Mice / Cities / Countryside

BOOKS TO READ:
>*The Town Mouse and the Country Mouse* by Helen Craig (Candlewick Press, 1992).
>*A Weekend in the Country* by Lee Lorenz (Prentice-Hall, 1985).
>*Come a Tide* by George Ella Lyon (Orchard Books, 1990).

MATERIALS: Hand puppets: city mouse (wearing a fancy bow tie), country mouse (wearing blue jeans), dog (with a moveable mouth); props: plastic food (including bread, cheese, dried beans, brownies, cookies, cupcakes); Velcro; hot glue gun and glue sticks; two cardboard bases for plastic food; hand puppet stage.

SETUP: Use Velcro to attach the bow tie and the blue jeans. Hot-glue the plastic food onto the cardboard bases (one base should contain the bread, cheese, and dried beans; the other base should contain the brownies, cookies, and cupcakes). Use your left hand for the country mouse and your right hand for the city mouse.

THE SHOW

[*The setting is the home of the country mouse.*]

COUNTRY MOUSE.
[*Country Mouse enters at stage left and stops, remaining at stage left.*] My cousin from the city. Welcome to my home here in the country.

CITY MOUSE.
[*City Mouse enters at stage right and walks over to the country mouse.*] It is so nice to be here in the country with the fresh air.

COUNTRY MOUSE.
Let's have dinner outside and enjoy the fresh air. We will have a picnic. I have some beans, bread, and cheese.

CITY MOUSE.
[*He looks at the bread.*] Why, this bread is moldy. [*He sniffs the cheese.*] The cheese stinks. [*He makes the motions of chewing on the beans and spitting them out.*] The beans are dry and have no taste.

COUNTRY MOUSE.
This is what we eat in the country every day. It is not real tasty, but it is filling. What do you like to eat?

CITY MOUSE.
Come with me to the city and I'll show you. [*Mice exit.*]

[*Scene change: remove the base containing the bread, cheese, and dried beans, and replace it with fake cupcakes, brownies, and cookies glued to a base. Mice enter.*]

CITY MOUSE.
Look at all the things we can eat: cupcakes, cookies, brownies.

COUNTRY MOUSE.
[*He makes motions of eating the food as he says:*] This is fine food. It tastes so good. Yes, your food is much better. My tummy is going to be so full. I'll have to buy some new pants. My old ones won't fit anymore.

YOU.
[*Make the sound of a dog that is barking offstage.*]

CITY MOUSE.
Run for your life! [*He exits.*]

[*Take the city mouse puppet off your hand and put on the dog puppet. Dog enters and lunges for the country mouse. The dog rips the clothes off the country mouse. The country mouse squeaks and exits, with the dog right behind him.*]

[*Take the country mouse off your hand and put on the city mouse. The city mouse and the dog enter. Onstage, the dog pulls off the city mouse's clothes, and they both exit.*]

[*Take the dog puppet off your hand and put on the country mouse. Mice enter without their clothes.*]

COUNTRY MOUSE.
I'm going back to the country. This place is too dangerous for me.

CITY MOUSE.
Stay here. The dog is gone.

COUNTRY MOUSE.
So are my clothes. I'm going home. My house is not fancy. But I don't have to worry about a dog. I can eat in peace and quiet.

YOU.
[*Make the sound of a dog that is barking offstage. Mice exit.*]

The Fisherman and His Wife

SUBJECT: Folktales

BOOKS TO READ: Any folktale.

MATERIALS: Hand puppets: wife, husband; clothing for the puppets (squares of fabric): floral-pattern dress, purple robe, emperor's robe (oriental-pattern fabric), golden robe of the Pope; sequined fish (made of cardboard); cutout pictures: cottage, castle, Roman Catholic church, oriental temple or emperor's palace; book rings; dowel; cardboard; sequins; white glue; cardboard-box stage.

SETUP: Decorate the cardboard-box stage as a room. Place the cardboard-box stage on a table. Place a chair to the left side of the table (for you to sit in, facing your audience, during the performance).

Punch two holes in each of the pictures; punch two holes in the cardboard box, near the top, front edge of the opening that will be facing the audience (each set of two holes must be the same distance apart). Attach the pictures to the box with the book rings (when you begin the show, the pictures should be flipped up on top of the box).

Cut a hole in the middle of each square of fabric (large enough that the fabric fits over the puppet's head). Place the clothes on a chair to the left of the chair you sit in during the performance. Stack them in the order you will need them, with the floral-pattern dress on top.

Cut out a fish shape from the cardboard and glue on sequins. Attach a dowel to the cardboard fish. Give the fish to the person in the audience who is closest to you, with instructions to hold it up whenever the fisherman catches the fish or calls up the fish.

Put your right hand through the back of the stage, and put the wife puppet on your right hand (she performs from this position in the box stage during the entire skit). Place the fisherman puppet on your left hand (he stands on your lap).

THE SHOW

YOU.
Once upon a time, there lived a poor fisherman and his wife. They lived in a shack by the sea. Every day the man went fishing, so they could have something to eat. Now one day he caught a big fish. [*Lean the fisherman out toward the audience and move his body back as if he were pulling up a fish.*]

FISH.
Put me back. I'll give you anything you wish. Put me back.

FISHERMAN.
Why, it's a talking fish. It's a special fish. Oh, we don't need anything. But I will put you back just because you are a talking fish. [*Person holding the fish puts it back in his or her lap.*]

[*Move the fisherman over to his wife in the stage. They kiss with a loud smacking sound.*]

WIFE.
Hi, dear. Catch anything?

FISHERMAN.
Yes, I did catch one, but I threw him back. He was a talking fish. Said we could have anything we want, but we don't need anything.

WIFE.
What? Why, look at this place. You go back and ask for a cottage—with a garden.

FISHERMAN.
Now that would be nice. I'll go ask him. [*Move the fisherman to the left and out toward the audience.*]

FISHERMAN.
Flounder, flounder in the sea. Come, oh come, come to me.

FISH.
What do you want? [*Fish is held up by the person in the audience.*]

FISHERMAN.
My wife and I would like a cottage with a garden.

FISH.
Go home. It's already there. [*The fish is pulled back into the manipulator's lap.*]

YOU.
[*Move the fisherman back to the stage.*] And when he got home, there was a cottage with a garden. [*Flip the first picture hanging on the stage box, to reveal the picture of a cottage with a garden. The pictures are resting on the top of the stage, and the fisherman pulls the picture down for the audience to see.*] And a new dress for his wife. [*The fisherman picks up the flowered dress and slips it over his wife's head.*]

FISHERMAN.
You look nice, dear.

WIFE.
Thank you.

YOU.
They lived that way for about a week, and then the wife said, "You know what I want?"

FISHERMAN.
What?

WIFE.
I want to live in a castle.

FISHERMAN.
Oh, the cottage is fine. We don't need a castle.

WIFE.
I want to live in a castle. You go tell that fish. Go on. [*The fisherman moves out and to the left.*]

FISHERMAN.
Flounder, flounder in the sea. Come, oh come, come to me.

FISH.
What do you want?

FISHERMAN.
My wife would like to live in a castle.

FISH.
Go home. She is already there. [*Move the fisherman back to the stage.*]

YOU.
And when he got home, there was a huge castle [*fisherman flips down the picture of the castle*] and the royal purple robes for her majesty. [*Fisherman takes off the flowered dress and replaces it with the royal purple robe.*]

FISHERMAN.
You look lovely, dear.

WIFE.
Thank you.

YOU.
They lived that way for about a week, and then she said, "You know what I want?"

FISHERMAN.
What?

WIFE.
I want to be the emperor.

FISHERMAN.
Being your majesty in the castle is enough. You don't need to be an emperor.

WIFE.
I want to be an emperor. You go tell that fish. Go on. [*Move fisherman out toward the audience.*]

FISHERMAN.
Flounder, flounder in the sea. Come, oh come, come to me.

FISH.
What does she want now?

FISHERMAN.
Oh, she wants to be the emperor.

FISH.
Go home. She already is. [*Move the fisherman back to the stage.*]

YOU.
And when he got home, there was a temple fit for an emperor [*the fisherman flips down the oriental temple picture*] and the new robes of her imperial highness, the emperor. [*The fisherman removes the purple robe and replaces it with a robe of oriental-print fabric.*] They lived that way for about a week, and then she said, "You know what I want?"

FISHERMAN.
What?

WIFE.
I want to be the Pope.

FISHERMAN.
Oh, no, you cannot be the Pope.

WIFE.
Yes, I want to be the Pope. You go tell that fish. Go on. [*Move the fisherman out to the left and toward the audience.*]

FISHERMAN.
Flounder, flounder in the sea. Come, oh come, come to me.

FISH.
What does she want now?

FISHERMAN.
She wants to be the Pope.

FISH.
Go home. She already is. [*Move the fisherman back to the stage.*]

YOU.
And when he got home, there was a huge Catholic church [*the fisherman flips down the picture of the church*] and the golden robes of the Pope. [*He removes the emperor robe from his wife and replaces it with the Pope's robe.*] They lived that way for about a week, and then she said, "You know what I want?"

FISHERMAN.
What?

WIFE.
I want to be like God.

FISHERMAN.
Oh, no you cannot do that.

WIFE.
Yes, I want to make the sun rise and set like God does.

FISHERMAN.
No, you cannot do that.

WIFE.
I want to be like God. Now you go tell that fish. Go on. [*Move the fisherman out to the left toward the audience.*]

FISHERMAN.

Flounder, flounder in the sea. Come, oh come, come to me.

FISH.

What does she want now?

FISHERMAN.

She wants—she wants to be like God.

FISH.

Go home. She is back in her hut. [*Move the fisherman back to the stage.*]

YOU.

And when he got back, all the beautiful buildings were gone [*the fisherman flips the pictures back up on top of the box stage*], and all the beautiful clothes were gone [*he takes the golden robe off his wife*], and they lived in that little hut for the rest of their lives—the fisherman and his wife.

The Gingerbread Boy

SUBJECT: Boys / Food / Foxes

BOOKS TO READ:
  Matthew and Tilly by Rebecca Jones (E. P. Dutton, 1991).
  Rosie's Walk by Pat Hutchins (Macmillan, 1968).

MATERIALS: Hand puppets: old lady, gingerbread boy, cow, dog, fox; hand puppet stage.

SETUP: Place the gingerbread boy puppet on the playboard at stage right (lay him down flat).

THE SHOW

OLD LADY.
[*Old Lady enters at stage left.*] I'm going to make my husband a fine gingerbread boy. That will be a nice treat for him. [*She walks to stage right and moves her hands over the gingerbread boy with appropriate cookie-making motions.*] Chocolate chips for your eyes, a raisin for your nose, and a red cherry for your mouth. That should make the gingerbread taste extra special. Now, into the oven with you. [*She slides the gingerbread boy a little to the right on the playboard and walks to left and offstage. She says (from offstage),* "Henry, where are you? I've baked you a big cookie."]

GINGERBREAD BOY.
[*Pull the gingerbread boy offstage with your right hand. He enters at stage right.*] Oh, it is hot in that oven. I thought that I was going to burn up in there. I feel better being out here.

OLD LADY.
[*Old Lady enters at stage left.*] Gingerbread boy, how did you get out of that oven? Come here. You will make a good snack for my husband.

GINGERBREAD BOY.

Oh no, not me. [*He runs to stage right as the old lady chases him, then back to stage left, with her still in pursuit, and then back to stage right.*] Run, run as fast as you can. You can't catch me, I'm the gingerbread man. [*He runs offstage. The old lady follows him offstage.*]

[*Drop the old lady puppet off your hand and put on the dog puppet. Enter the gingerbread boy at stage right and the dog at stage left.*]

DOG.

Woof, woof! A doggie treat. Come here gingerbread boy. It's you I want to eat.

GINGERBREAD BOY.

Run, run as fast as you can. You can't catch me, I'm the gingerbread man. [*He runs to stage right as the dog chases him, then back to stage left, with the dog still in pursuit, and then back to stage right. He runs offstage. The dog follows him offstage.*]

[*Drop the dog puppet off your hand and put on the cow puppet. Enter the gingerbread boy at stage right and the cow at stage left.*]

COW.

Moo, moo! You are good food for a cow. Come over here. I'm going to eat you right now.

GINGERBREAD BOY.

Run, run as fast as you can. You can't catch me, I'm the gingerbread man. [*He runs to stage right as the cow chases him, then back to stage left, with the cow still in pursuit, and then back to stage right. He runs offstage. The cow follows him offstage.*]

[*Drop the cow puppet off your hand and put on the fox puppet. Enter the gingerbread boy at stage right and the fox at stage left.*]

GINGERBREAD BOY.

Oh please, Mr. Fox, don't eat me. Everyone is chasing me and I can't go any farther because of the river.

FOX.

I won't eat you. Who is chasing you?

GINGERBREAD BOY.

The old lady, and her dog, and now her cow. They all want to eat me.

FOX.

I can take you across the river. Just jump on my tail

GINGERBREAD BOY.

Are you sure you can get me across the river?

FOX.

[*Smoothly*] I know I can do it. Just jump onto my tail. [*Place the gingerbread boy on the fox's tail and move them slowly toward stage left.*] My tail is going under the water. Jump onto my back. [*Move the gingerbread boy onto the fox's back.*] My back is going under the water. Jump onto my head. [*Move the gingerbread boy onto the fox's head. Snap the fox's head as you jump the fox up and pull the gingerbread boy down and offstage.*]

FOX.

Mmm, mmm. What a wonderful treat for a fox to eat. You can catch the gingerbread man. It isn't easy. But it's worth it! Mmm, mmm, good! [*Fox takes a bow and exits at stage left.*]

Goldilocks and the Three Bears

SUBJECT: Fairytales / Homes / Bears

BOOKS TO READ:
Teddy Bears Cure a Cold by Susanna Gretz (Four Winds Press, 1984).
Corduroy by Don Freeman (Viking Press, 1968).
A House Is a House for Me by Mary Ann Hoberman (Viking Children's Books, 1978).

MATERIALS: Glove puppet with three fingers and a thumb (dark-colored felt, needle, thread); Goldilocks "head" (one-inch-diameter pink pompom, curly yellow chenille, two wiggly eyes, red felt); three small stuffed bears (available at craft stores); hot glue gun and glue sticks.

SETUP: On a piece of felt, trace your right hand with your fingers spread apart—except for your forefinger and your middle finger, which should be close together (thereby forming three fingers—the larger finger is for Papa Bear). Cut out this pattern on two pieces of felt, simultaneously. Sew the two pieces of felt together. Hot-glue a small stuffed bear to each finger of the glove. Make the Goldilocks head and attach it to the thumb of the glove, on the side of the glove opposite from the bears (see below).

You can stand or sit, facing your audience. When Goldilocks is onstage, put the glove puppet on your right hand (with the bears facing you). When the bears are onstage, place the glove on your left hand (with Goldilocks facing you).

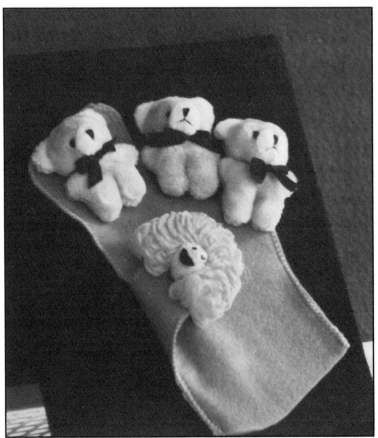

THE SHOW

YOU.

Once upon a time, Goldilocks went for a walk in the woods. She saw a house, and knocked on the door. When no one answered, she walked into the house. The three bears who lived there had gone to Texas to see the rodeo. [*Pause while the audience reacts to the last statement.*]

They didn't go to Texas? They didn't get to see the rodeo? That's right, they just went for a walk. Goldilocks walked over to the kitchen table. The three bears had left their lunch on the table. It was Spam on white bread. [*Pause while the audience reacts to the last statement.*]

They didn't have any Spam? They didn't have any white bread? It was their breakfast? It was porridge? All right. Goldilocks tasted the porridge in Papa Bear's bowl. [*To represent a bowl, form a circle with the forefinger and thumb of your left hand. To pantomime Goldilocks eating, bend your right thumb down into the bowl created by your left hand.*] It was too hot. She tasted the porridge in Mama Bear's bowl. It was too cold. She tasted the porridge in Baby Bear's bowl. It was just right. She ate it all up. Then Goldilocks sat down to watch TV. [*Pause while the audience reacts.*]

She didn't sit down? They didn't have a TV? She did sit down on Papa Bear's chair. [*To represent a chair, make a fist with your left hand. To pantomime Goldilocks sitting on a chair, rest your right thumb on the back of your left fist.*] It was too hard. Then she sat down on Mama Bear's chair. It was too soft. Finally, she sat down on Baby Bear's chair. It was just right, but then it broke all to pieces. Next, Goldilocks went outside to the swimming pool. [*Pause while the audience reacts.*]

They didn't have a pool? She went upstairs to the bedrooms? That's right. First she lay down on Papa Bear's bed. [*To represent a bed, use the inside of your left forearm. To pantomime Goldilocks lying on a bed, rest your right thumb on the inside of your left forearm.*] It was too hard. Then she lay down on Mama Bear's bed. It was too soft. Finally, she lay down on Baby Bear's bed. It was just right, and she fell asleep.

Now the three bears came back from their walk. Papa Bear looked at his porridge and said, "Who stuck their fingers in my porridge?" Mama Bear looked at her porridge and said, "Who stuck their tongue in my porridge?" Baby Bear said, "Somebody ate my porridge all up."

Then Papa Bear said, "Somebody has been sitting in my chair." Mama Bear said, "Somebody put their dirty feet on my chair." Baby Bear said, "Somebody sat in my chair and broke it all to pieces."

Upstairs, Papa Bear said, "Somebody has been jumping on my bed." Mama Bear said, "Somebody has been messing up my bed." Baby Bear said, "Here she is in my bed." [*Fold your left thumb down in front of the bears, and bend your fingers so that the bears are looking down on her.*]

Goldilocks woke up, took one look at those bears, and ran home. You'll never guess what she did. The next time she went over there, she took them some Spam sandwiches.

The Lion and the Mouse

SUBJECT: Friends / Lions / Mice

BOOKS TO READ:
  Five Bad Boys, Billy Que, and the Dustdobbin by Susan Patron (Orchard Books, 1992).
  A Bargain for Frances by Russell Hoban (Harper & Row, 1970).
  Patrick and Ted by Geoffrey Hayes (Four Winds Press, 1984).

MATERIALS: Rod puppets: mouse and lion; hand puppet stage; small net.

SETUP: Hold the lion puppet in your right hand and the mouse puppet in your left hand.

THE SHOW

[*The show begins with the mouse at center stage.*]

LION.
[*Lion enters at stage right and pounces on the mouse.*] Gotcha! What a tasty treat I have for my supper! You will slide down easy.

MOUSE.
Please let me go. I'm only a small morsel. I'll be your friend.

LION.
I don't need a friend. I'm the king of the animals. I'm very powerful, and I sure don't need a little pip-squeak like you for a friend. Oh, all right. I'll let you go this time. Stay away from lions. You hear?!

MOUSE.
Thank you so much. If you ever need a friend, I'll be your friend. Everybody needs friends.

LION.
Bah! Go on! I already told you. I don't need friends.

[*Mouse exits. Put him down and pick up a net. Walk the Lion along the playboard and toss the net over him.*]

LION.
Hey, what's going on? I'm the king of the beasts. You can't do this to me. Let me go!

MOUSE.
[*Mouse enters at stage left.*] I'm here to help you. It's me, your friend.

LION.
I don't need a friend. I need to get this net off me. I can't move. [*Lion pushes against the net.*]

MOUSE.
I can bite this string in two. Just hold still. You're making me crazy.

LION.
Okay! Okay! Just hurry up. [*Mouse pulls the net off the lion.*]

MOUSE.
There you go, my friend. You're free. No more net.

LION.
Thank you, my friend. I didn't know that such a little mouse like you could do such a big thing as getting that net off me. Thank you for being here when I needed you.

MOUSE.
You're welcome. That's what friends are for. I'm glad to help when I can. [*Mouse exits.*]

LION.
And I kept telling him I didn't need a friend. From now on, I'm going to stop and taste my words before I let them past my teeth. Growl!

The Little Red Hen

SUBJECT: Helping / Sharing

BOOKS TO READ:
Jerome the Babysitter by Eileen Christelow (Clarion Books, 1985).
I Hate English by Ellen Levine (Scholastic, 1989).
The Little Red Hen by Margot Zemach (Farrar, Straus & Giroux, 1983).

MATERIALS: Hand, finger, or rod puppets: one Little Red Hen and several dogs, cats, pigs, and cows; recording: "The Little Red Hen Operetta" [*Puppet Parade* by Sharron Lucky (Melody House, n.d.), available on cassette and LP in teacher supply stores and music stores]. (No puppet stage is required.)

SETUP: See the finger puppet patterns on pages 54–57, or the glove puppet pattern on page 58.

THE SHOW

This is an all-music rendition in song performed by the audience. You are the director. After the children have placed the puppets on their hands, group the cats together, the dogs together, and so on, in a large circle, so they can watch each other perform. Instruct them to listen carefully to the recording and to watch you, the director, for their cues as to when they should move their puppets as they sing in this operetta. The children use their puppets to pantomime the actions of the story. Start the recording.

If there are not enough puppets for each child to have one, the available puppets may be used by one group of children and then passed to the next group during the scenes performed by the Little Red Hen. Keep the Red Hen puppet on one person's hand throughout the show.

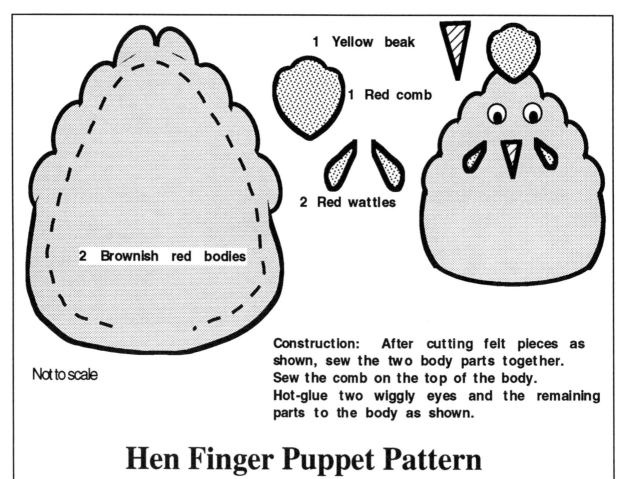

Construction: After cutting felt pieces as shown, sew the two body parts together. Sew the comb on the top of the body. Hot-glue two wiggly eyes and the remaining parts to the body as shown.

Hen Finger Puppet Pattern

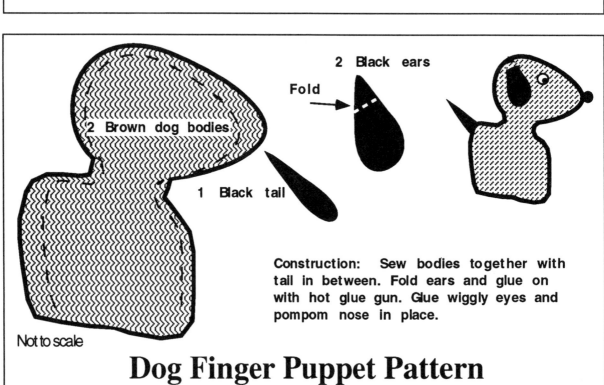

Construction: Sew bodies together with tail in between. Fold ears and glue on with hot glue gun. Glue wiggly eyes and pompom nose in place.

Dog Finger Puppet Pattern

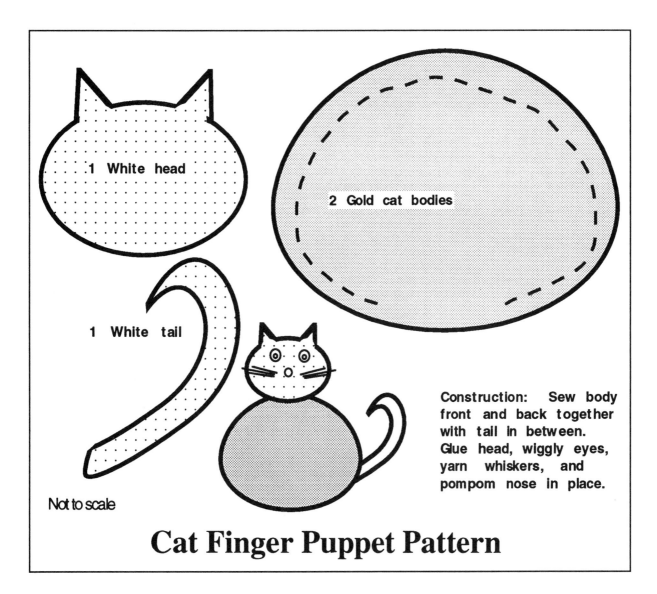

1 White head

2 Gold cat bodies

1 White tail

Not to scale

Construction: Sew body front and back together with tail in between. Glue head, wiggly eyes, yarn whiskers, and pompom nose in place.

Cat Finger Puppet Pattern

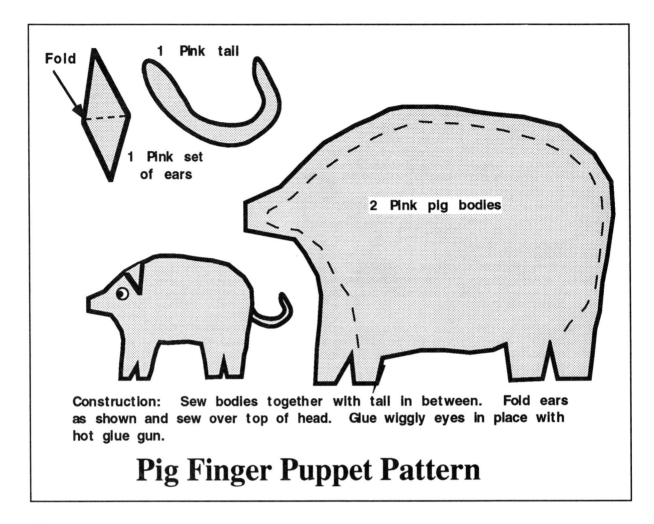

Fold

1 Pink tail

1 Pink set of ears

2 Pink pig bodies

Construction: Sew bodies together with tail in between. Fold ears as shown and sew over top of head. Glue wiggly eyes in place with hot glue gun.

Pig Finger Puppet Pattern

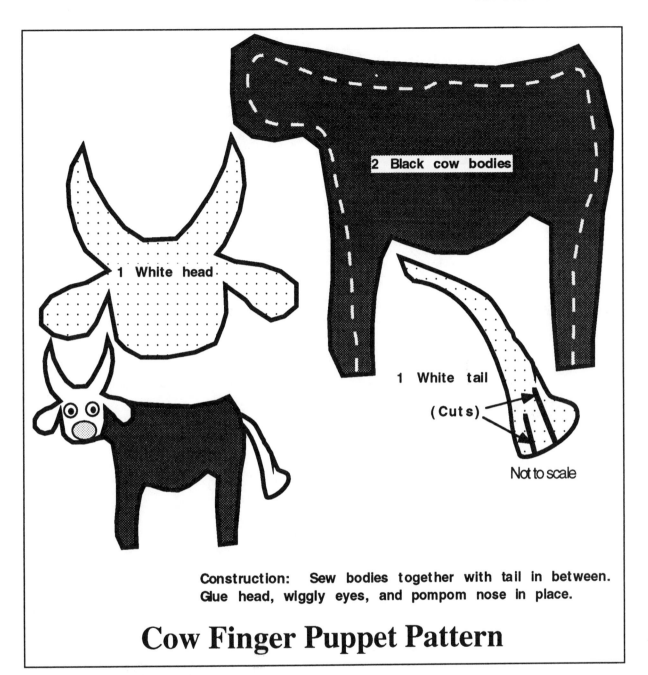

1 White head

2 Black cow bodies

1 White tail

(Cuts)

Not to scale

Construction: Sew bodies together with tail in between. Glue head, wiggly eyes, and pompom nose in place.

Cow Finger Puppet Pattern

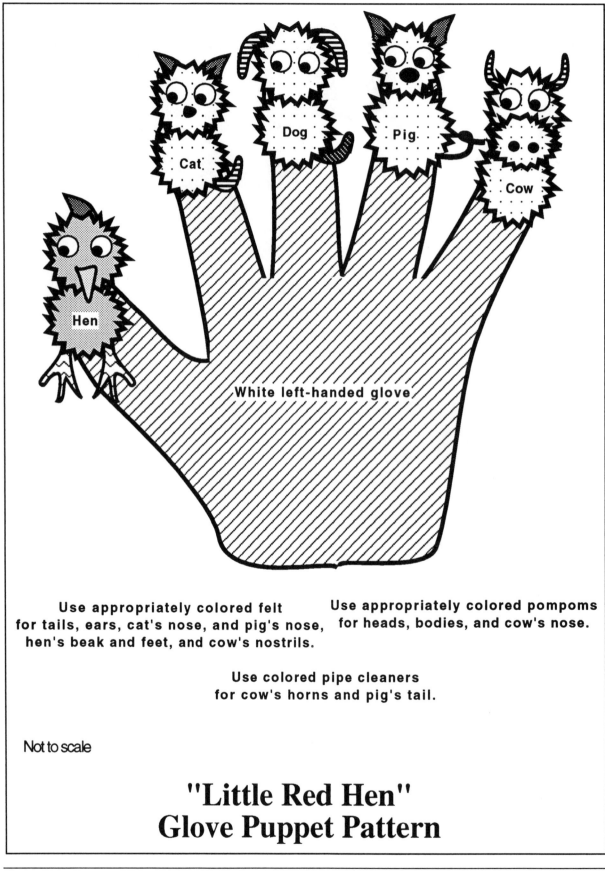

Use appropriately colored felt
for tails, ears, cat's nose, and pig's nose,
hen's beak and feet, and cow's nostrils.

Use appropriately colored pompoms
for heads, bodies, and cow's nose.

Use colored pipe cleaners
for cow's horns and pig's tail.

Not to scale

"Little Red Hen"
Glove Puppet Pattern

Little Red Riding Hood

SUBJECT: Wolves / Grandmothers

BOOKS TO READ:
> *The Wolf and the Seven Little Kids* by The Brothers Grimm (Larousse, c1977).
> *Mr. and Mrs. Pig's Evening Out* by Mary Rayner (Atheneum, c1976).

MATERIALS: Glove puppet (dark-colored felt, needle, thread, pompoms, chenille, wiggly eyes, felt) with the following characters: Little Red Riding Hood on the forefinger, the wolf on the middle finger, the woodsman on the ring finger, the grandmother on the pinkie finger, and the wolf dressed in the grandmother's nightgown on the thumb (attach the wolf dressed in grandmother's nightgown to the side of the glove opposite from the other characters—see below); hot glue gun and glue sticks.

SETUP: On a piece of felt, trace your right hand with your fingers spread apart. Cut out this pattern on two pieces of felt, simultaneously. Sew the two pieces of felt together. Make the characters and hot-glue them to the fingers and thumb of the glove. When you put the glove puppet on your right hand, the wolf dressed in the grandmother's nightgown should be facing you.

THE SHOW

YOU.
> Once upon a time, Little Red Riding Hood's mother told her to take some money and go shopping at the mall. [*Wiggle your forefinger (Little Red Riding Hood) and pause while the audience reacts.*]

She didn't tell her to go shopping? She told her to go to her grandmother's house? Oh, that's right, she did tell her to go to her grandmother's house—and to take a basket of goodies with her. So Little Red Riding Hood walked all around town, past the grocery store, past the . . . [*Wiggle your forefinger and pause while the audience reacts.*]

She didn't walk all around town? She went through the woods? Okay. Her mother told her to say "Hi" to everyone— even the wolf—and also to be nice to the wolf. [*Wiggle your forefinger and pause while the audience reacts.*]

She didn't say that? She said not to talk to strangers? All right, she was walking through the woods. The wolf saw her, came up to her, and asked her where she was going. [*Wiggle your middle finger (the wolf).*] She told him that she was going shopping at the mall. [*Wiggle your forefinger and pause while the audience reacts.*]

She didn't say that? Oh, that's right, she told him she was going to her grandmother's house [*wiggle your forefinger*] because her grandmother was sick and she was taking her a basket of goodies. So the wolf ran off to go shopping at the mall. [*Wiggle your middle finger and pause while the audience reacts.*]

He didn't go shopping? He went to the grandmother's house? [*Wiggle your middle finger.*] That's right, he did go to the grandmother's house. Now, when the grandmother opened the door and saw the wolf, she became scared—so scared that she ran into a closet and locked the door. [*Wiggle your pinkie finger (the grandmother).*] Then the wolf dressed himself in the grandmother's nightie and cap and got into her bed. [*Bend down your thumb (the wolf dressed in grandmother's clothing) in front of your forefinger.*]

When Little Red Riding Hood got to her grandmother's house, she knocked on the door. The wolf said, "Nobody is home. Go away. We don't want to buy anything." [*Wiggle your thumb and pause while the audience reacts.*]

He didn't say that? He said that she should come right in? That's right. The wolf told her to come right in. So she went into the house and saw what looked like a watermelon lying in the bed. [*Wiggle your forefinger and pause while the audience reacts.*]

The wolf didn't look like a watermelon? The wolf looked like her grandmother? That's right. The wolf looked like her grandmother. She said, "Grandma,

what a big nose you have." [*Wiggle your forefinger and pause while the audience reacts.*]

She didn't say that? Oh, that's right. She said, "What big eyes you have." [*Wiggle your forefinger.*] "The better to see you with, my dear," said the wolf. [*Wiggle your thumb.*] "Grandma, what big hair you have," she said. [*Wiggle your forefinger and pause while the audience reacts.*]

She didn't say that? Oh, that's right. She said, "What big ears you have." [*Wiggle your forefinger.*] "The better to hear you with, my dear," said the wolf. [*Wiggle your thumb.*] "Grandma, what big teeth you have," she said. [*Wiggle your forefinger.*] "The better to eat you with, my dear," said the wolf. He leaped out of bed and chased Little Red Riding Hood. She screamed for help [*wiggle your forefinger*], and the school principal heard her and came running into the house to help. [*Pause while the audience reacts.*]

It wasn't the principal? It was a woodsman? That's right. It was a woodsman who came running into the house. He said to the wolf, "If you don't be a good boy, you are going to be expelled from school." [*Wiggle your ring finger (the woodsman).*]

The woodsman didn't threaten to expel the wolf? The woodsman chased the wolf back into the woods? That's right. He chased the wolf away. [*Wiggle your ring finger and your middle finger.*]

Then the grandmother stepped out of the closet. [*Wiggle your pinkie finger.*]

Then the grandmother and Little Red Riding Hood sat down and ate the goodies in the basket. They were sure tired after all that excitement. [*Wiggle your forefinger and your pinkie finger.*]

Thank you for helping me with this story.

The Monkey and the Crocodile

SUBJECT: Monkeys / Crocodiles

BOOKS TO READ:
Little Gorilla by Ruth Bornstein (Houghton Mifflin, 1976).
Ernst by Elisa Kleben (E. P. Dutton, 1989).

MATERIALS: Hand puppets: monkey, crocodile; props: rock or fake rock, artificial leaves; hand puppet stage.

SETUP: Attach artificial leaves (to represent trees) at the top of the scrim using clothespins or paper clips. Place a rock or a fake rock on the playboard at stage left. Put the crocodile puppet on your left hand and the monkey puppet on your right hand.

THE SHOW

[*Enter the crocodile at stage left and place the monkey at the top of the scrim at stage right (the monkey is sitting in the trees).*]

CROCODILE.
Oh, I'm so hungry! There must be something around here that I can eat. [*It looks around and up and then at the audience.*] Ah! A monkey. I would like to catch a monkey and eat him. [*It walks back and forth across the stage.*] I want to catch that monkey. How can I catch that monkey? Oh, I know. [*To the monkey:*] Hey, monkey toes! Do you want to go to the island to get more fruit to eat? Come with me.

MONKEY.
I want to go over there, but I can't swim. How can I come with you if I can't swim?

CROCODILE.
I'll carry you on my back. [*Move the monkey out of the trees, onto the playboard, and onto the crocodile's back. Start moving the crocodile to stage right.*]

MONKEY.
This is a nice ride on your green hide.

CROCODILE.
How do you like this? [*Pull the crocodile and monkey down, offstage, for a moment and then bring them back up onto the playboard at center stage.*]

MONKEY.
Don't do that! I told you that I can't swim. Why did you do that?

CROCODILE.
Because I'm hungry. First I'm going to drown you. Then I'm going to eat you.

MONKEY.
I wish you would have told me that before. I left my heart in the tree—my heart is the tastiest part of me.

CROCODILE.
Oh! Then we'll go back and get it right now!

MONKEY.
We are so close to the island. Take me there first, then we can go back.

CROCODILE.
No, no, no. First we go back to the tree to get your heart, then we will see about going to the island.

MONKEY.

All right, crocodile nose. Have it your way. Take me back to my tree. [*Move the crocodile and the monkey to stage right. Lift the monkey off the crocodile's back and swing him to the back of the scrim and then up to the top, so that he is sitting in the tree.*] My heart is up here. If you want it, come and get it. Ha, ha, ha.

CROCODILE.

I'll get you some day, monkey toes. Watch your front, and watch your back—because I will get you. [*The crocodile exits at stage left.*]

MONKEY.

I'm going to move because I don't want that crocodile to get me. [*Move the monkey over to the center of the top of the scrim.*] This is a great tree to live in. Why, I can jump from my tree to that rock to the island. Yes! [*Bring the monkey down from the tree, behind the scrim, up onto the rock at stage left on the playboard, and then jump him over to the right side of the playboard.*] What a great spot. I can eat fruit on this island every day. [*Jump the monkey back to the rock and back into the tree.*]

CROCODILE.

[*The crocodile enters at stage left.*] I see where monkey toes is living now, and I see how he goes to the rock and then to the island. [*Duck the crocodile under the playboard and jump the monkey down from the tree to the rock and then over to stage right. Bring the crocodile up onto the playboard.*] I'll catch him when he comes back to his tree. [*Drape the crocodile across the rock with his head facing toward the monkey.*]

MONKEY.

It is time to go home. Say, something is wrong with that rock. It looks different. Hello, rock! Hello, rock! Hello, rock! Why don't you answer me when I call?

CROCODILE.

Yes, monkey toes! What do you want?

MONKEY.

Oh, it's you, crocodile nose.

CROCODILE.

Yes, it is me. I'm waiting here to eat you!

MONKEY.

You caught me this time. There is no other way I can get home. Go ahead and open your mouth and I'll jump in. [*Open the crocodile's mouth wide. Jump the monkey onto the crocodile's head, then back behind the scrim, then up to the top of the scrim to the tree.*] Ha, ha, ha!

CROCODILE.

Oh, I give up. You are a very smart monkey. I will not bother you anymore.

MONKEY.

Thank you crocodile nose, but I will be watching for you just the same.

CROCODILE.

I guess I'll eat spiders for supper.

[*The crocodile takes a bow, then the monkey takes a bow. Both puppets exit at stage left.*]

The Nutcracker and the Mouse King

SUBJECT: Christmas / Gifts

BOOKS TO READ:
Paul's Christmas Birthday by Carol Carrick (Morrow, 1978).
Koala Christmas by Lisa Bassett (Dutton Children's Books, 1991).

MATERIALS: Hand puppets: Uncle Drosselmeyer, Fritz, Clara, Mouse King, Prince; rod puppets: King Winter, Queen Winter, Sugar Plum Princess, nutcracker, stretch-neck monster; additional puppets for the audience: two "humanettes" (doll-like figures without heads to tie around your neck—so that your head becomes the head of the figure), two small marionettes, five pop-up puppets, holiday hand puppets with a bell sewn on each puppet (one for each child); three wooden Christmas tree ornament nutcracker soldiers (with pull strings to raise and lower soldiers' arms and legs); three wooden Christmas tree ornament Mouse King soldiers (with pull strings to raise and lower soldiers' arms and legs), props: toy bed, toy nutcracker, toy hobby horse, child's shoe, candy house; recording: *The Nutcracker Suite*; large dowel; two broom holders; hand puppet stage.

SETUP: Put each set of three soldiers on a tandem device so that you can manipulate each set with one hand; tie the pull strings together. Attach a broom holder to the playboard at stage left and stage right. Attach a large dowel to the bottom of the toy bed (so that it can be picked up and turned around during the performance). Place the dowel into the broom holder.

THE SHOW

SCENE 1:

[*Play the overture from* The Nutcracker Suite. *Place a toy bed on the playboard at stage right. Put the Uncle Drosselmeyer puppet, with a toy hobby horse in his hands, on your left hand, and the Fritz puppet on your right hand.*]

UNCLE DROSSELMEYER.
[*Uncle Drosselmeyer enters at stage left.*] Fritz? Where are you, Fritz? I have your Christmas present.

FRITZ.
[*Fritz enters at stage right.*] Here I am, Uncle Drosselmeyer.

UNCLE DROSSELMEYER.
Merry Christmas, Fritz. Here is a present from me. I hope that you enjoy it.

FRITZ.
[*Fritz takes the hobby horse from his uncle.*] Thank you, Uncle Drosselmeyer. I love it. I'll ride it right now.

[*Uncle Drosselmeyer exits at stage left while Fritz rides the hobby horse back and forth across the stage and then exits at stage right. Put down the hobby horse, take the Fritz puppet off your hand, and put on the Clara puppet. Put the toy nutcracker into Uncle Drosselmeyer's hands.*]

UNCLE DROSSELMEYER.
[*Uncle Drosselmeyer enters at stage left.*] Clara? Oh, Clara? Where are you? I have your Christmas present.

CLARA.
[*Clara enters at stage right.*] Here I am. [*She takes the toy nutcracker from her uncle.*] What is it?

UNCLE DROSSELMEYER.

It's a nutcracker. You put a nut into its mouth, pull down the handle, and the nut is cracked. Do you want to try it?

CLARA.

Yes. Put the nut in here. Pull down the handle like this. [*Clara pulls down the handle.*] It works great. Thank you very much.

UNCLE DROSSELMEYER.

You're welcome. Enjoy your Christmas Eve. I'll see you tomorrow for Christmas dinner. [*He exits at stage left.*]

[*Take the Uncle Drosselmeyer puppet off your hand and put on the Fritz puppet.*]

CLARA.

What a wonderful present. I can't believe this nutcracker is really mine.

FRITZ.

[*Fritz enters at stage left.*] What is it? Another one of your dolls that does nothing? Does it just sit there?

CLARA.

No, it doesn't just sit there. It does something very special.

FRITZ.

Like what? Wet its pants?

CLARA.

No, it doesn't wet its pants. Look. I put a nut in its mouth, pull down the handle, and the nut cracks. [*Clara pulls down the handle.*] Pretty special, isn't it?

FRITZ.

Let me see that thing. There. Crack that nut. [*Fritz hits the toy nutcracker.*] Hah!

CLARA.

You broke it. You broke it. It is my favorite toy, and you broke it. I just got it for Christmas.

FRITZ.

Well, take it back to the store and exchange it.

CLARA.

No, I don't want to take it back to the store. I want to keep it. Now it is broken and I don't know how to fix it.

FRITZ.

Just do like the song says—"Don't worry, be *crabby.*"

CLARA.

That isn't what the song says, and you know it. Now you're acting like a brother—without the "r".

FRITZ.

What is that supposed to mean?

CLARA.

You are being a *bother.* Now leave me alone. Go to bed. Tomorrow is Christmas. I hope that you dream about something sweet, because you need to sweeten yourself.

FRITZ.

I hope that you dream about rats and mice. [*Fritz exits at stage left.*]

CLARA.

Go to bed, little nutcracker. It's Christmas Eve. Good night. [*Clara picks up the toy nutcracker and places it in the bed.*] I'll see you in the morning. I hope that your jaw will be all right. You are such a fine soldier. I think Fritz thought that you should belong to him. But you are mine. Good night, little nutcracker, good night. [*Clara lies down on the bed and goes to sleep.*]

[*Take your hand out of the Clara puppet, leaving her on the bed. Pick up the bed using the dowel, turn the bed around, and carry the bed offstage while saying: "Clara fell asleep. She dreamed about a nutcracker, a Prince, a Sugar Plum Princess, and a Mouse King—all of whom lived in Sugar Plum Land." Put down the bed, the Clara puppet, and the toy nutcracker.*]

SCENE 2:

[*Pick up the King Winter and Queen Winter rod puppets and hold them up over your head so that the audience can see them above the top of the scrim as they say their lines.*]

KING WINTER.
What do you think about the weather, Queen Winter?

QUEEN WINTER.
The Mouse King is looking for a break in the weather, so he can get to Sugar Plum Land. He is waiting for the opportunity to capture the Sugar Plum Princess. Then he and his mice will eat all the candy buildings.

KING WINTER.
Opportunity knocks only once. Trouble is more persistent.

QUEEN WINTER.
Oh, the Mouse King is trouble all right. He will do anything to get that candy. Is there something we can do to stop him?

KING WINTER.
Clara is on her way to Sugar Plum Land, so we don't want to make the weather too bad. We don't want Clara to get hurt.

QUEEN WINTER.
If the Mouse King would just stay where he lives and mind his own business, there wouldn't be any trouble.

KING WINTER.
There are two reasons why he won't mind his own business: number one, he has no mind, and number two, he has no business.

QUEEN WINTER.
Now, King Winter, you know that the Mouse King is a bully. He is going to hurt everyone he meets. I really think that we should try to stop him.

KING WINTER.
If he does eat all the candy, he will get sick with a big stomachache. Don't worry, someone will be clever enough to stop him.

[*King and Queen exit the stage.*]

SCENE 3:

[*Place the Nutcracker rod puppet into the broom holder (at stage left). Place the candy house on the playboard at stage right. Put the Mouse King puppet on your right hand and the Prince puppet on you left hand.*]

MOUSE KING.
[*Mouse King enters at stage right.*] All right, where is she? I'll get that Sugar Plum Princess, and then all the candy in Sugar Plum Land will be mine. Do you hear me? Mine. This land is your land. This land is my land. So stay on your land.

PRINCE.
[*Prince enters at stage left.*] What are you doing in Sugar Plum Land?

MOUSE KING.
I'm looking for the Sugar Plum Princess.

PRINCE.
I hope that some flabby tabby cat comes along and gobbles you up, Mouse King. A bully like you does not deserve all the candy that he wants.

MOUSE KING.
I'll finish you off, Prince. I'll change you into that nutcracker over there.

PRINCE.
You won't get away with this.

MOUSE KING.
Oh, won't I? Into the nutcracker with you! [*Pushes the Prince toward the nutcracker. Exit the Prince at stage left.*] Mice, into battle with you! [*Mouse King exits at stage right.*]

[*Play "The March of the Nutcracker" from* The Nutcracker Suite. *Pick up the toy nutcracker soldiers (on a tandem device) with your left hand and the toy mice soldiers (on a tandem device) with your right hand. Enter the nutcracker soldiers at stage left and the mice soldiers at stage right. Move each set of soldiers back and forth, as they clash in battle to the music, pulling down the tied-together pull strings with your forefingers. During the battle, the Mouse King coaches his soldiers from offstage—yelling, "Come on mice! Hit them again!" Finally, the nutcracker soldiers push the mice soldiers offstage. The nutcracker soldiers yell, "We win! We win!" Stop the music. Put down the soldiers and put the Mouse King puppet on your right hand.]*

MOUSE KING.
> *[Mouse King enters at stage right.]* Nobody wants me in Sugar Plum Land. Maybe I should find some place to hide, some place where no one can find me. *[He exits at stage right.]*

[Take off the Mouse King puppet. Pick up the stretch-neck monster puppet and slip your right hand into his glove foot. Slide all the material up to the monster's neck. Grasp the rod with your left hand.]

MONSTER.
> *[Monster enters at stage right.]* I'm looking for the Mouse King. I think I see his eyes. *[It looks around.]* I think I see his nose. *[It looks to the right.]* I think I see his teeth. *[It looks to the left and moves to the left.]* I'm looking for the Mouse King. I think I see his feet. *[It moves to the left. Then shove the monster's head into the audience as the monster yells:]* He's here! *[Bring the monster back onto the playboard. Monster exits at stage left.]*

SCENE 4:

[Play "The Dance of the Sugar Plum Fairy" from The Nutcracker Suite. *Enter the Sugar Plum Princess rod puppet at stage left and make her dance to the music, manipulating the rods on her feet with one hand and holding the rod attached to her back with the other hand. After a minute or so, stop the music. Hold the Sugar Plum Princess puppet so that she is standing upright on the playboard.]*

MOUSE KING.
> *[Mouse King enters at stage right.]* Aha! *[He grabs the Sugar Plum Princess.]* I gotcha! You're mine now. You and all the candy in Sugar Plum Land are mine. This is a happy Christmas for me—I got what I wanted.

SUGAR PLUM PRINCESS.
> Oh, please let me go.

MOUSE KING.
> Oh, no! You are going to be my bride. All these candy buildings will be food for my kingdom of mice.

SUGAR PLUM PRINCESS.
> I'm not going to marry you. You are not very nice.

MOUSE KING.
> I'm a nice guy. I will *ask* you for the candy. Please, Sugar Plum Princess, may we eat these candy buildings?

SUGAR PLUM PRINCESS.
> No, you may not.

MOUSE KING.
> All right! That's it! You are out of here! *[Mouse Kings starts examining the candy house at stage right, with his back to stage left.]*

[Exit the Sugar Plum Princess. Put the Clara puppet on your left hand and pick up the child's shoe with her hands.]

CLARA.
> *[Clara enters at stage left and quietly walks over to the Mouse King, who has his back to her.]* Mouse King, you are through playing your tricks—forever. *[She hits him on the head with the shoe.]*

MOUSE KING.
> Oww!

[Clara hits the Mouse King again with the shoe and then drops it. Let the Mouse King fall offstage. Clara clasps her hands together. Put on the Prince puppet, keeping him offstage.]

NUTCRACKER.
> Please, let me out of here.

CLARA.
> Nutcracker, is that you talking? *[She looks at the nutcracker.]*

NUTCRACKER.
> It is me, the Prince. I'm trapped inside your Christmas toy. The Mouse King put me in here. Please get me out.

CLARA.
> Come on, Prince, come on out of there.

PRINCE.

[*Prince enters at stage left by the nut-cracker puppet and passes by Clara, moving toward stage right (hold the Clara puppet away from the playboard to let him pass by her).*] That was a tight squeeze. Thank you, Clara. Thank you.

CLARA.

This calls for a celebration, a party with music and dancing. Let the music begin.

[*Clara and the Prince bow and exit together at stage right. Take off the puppets and walk out in front of the stage.*]

YOU.

Now we need two volunteers to perform a Russian dance. Who would like to be a "humanette" puppet? [*Pick up the humanettes and put them on the children who volunteer. Show them how to manipulate the humanettes. Play "Trepak" (the Russian dance) from* The Nut-cracker Suite *and have the two children dance to the music. Take the humanettes off the volunteers.*] Now we need two volunteers to perform an Arabian dance. Who would like to perform with a marionette puppet? [*Play "Coffee" (the Arabian dance) and have the two children dance the marionettes to the music.*] Now we need two volunteers to perform a Chinese dance. Who would like to perform with a pop-up puppet? [*Play "Tea" (the Chinese dance) and have the children dance the pop-up puppets to the music.*] Now we all will perform "The Dance of the Toy Flutes." [*Distribute the hand puppets with jingle bells. Play "The Dance of the Toy Flutes" and have the children dance and jingle their hand puppets to the music.*] Now, everyone take a bow!

The Princess and the Pea

SUBJECT: Princes / Princesses / Fairytales

BOOKS TO READ:
> *Tumble Tower* by Anne Tyler (Orchard Books, 1993).
> *Princess Abigail and the Wonderful Hat* by Steven Kroll (Holiday House, 1991).
> *The Princess and the Frog* by Rachel Isadora (Greenwillow Books, 1989).

MATERIALS: Hand puppets: queen, prince (Andrew), princess (Sarah); props: 20 pieces of polyfoam covered with fabric and sewn together (the mattresses), toy cockroach, toy mouse; two dowels; hot glue gun and glue sticks; hand puppet stage.

SETUP: Hot-glue the dowels to the toy cockroach and the toy mouse. Place the mattresses at stage right. Put the prince puppet on your left hand and the queen puppet on your right hand.

THE SHOW

[*Andrew and the queen enter at stage left.*]

QUEEN.
Andrew, oh Andrew. Please help me with these mattresses. I want to be ready in case one of those fortune-hunting girls comes around, claiming to be a princess.

ANDREW.
You mean you want to have a bed ready for her? This one is so high. Why do you need so many mattresses on one bed?

QUEEN.
It's for the test. Go and get a dried green pea and put it under the mattresses. If that little pea bothers her while she is trying to sleep, we will know she is a real princess.

ANDREW.
While I get the green pea, you can dust the mattresses. [*He exits.*]

[*The queen wipes the mattresses. Pick up a mouse on a control stick and run it across the playboard. The queen screams. Run the mouse up and down the mattresses and back across the playboard. The queen chases the mouse. The mouse chases the queen and then exits. The queen continues to yell for help.*]

ANDREW.
What is wrong? Why are you yelling? What is the problem?

QUEEN.
There is a mouse in here. He must have a nest in one of the mattresses. A mouse. He scared me. He chased me!

ANDREW.
Oh, mother. A little mouse won't hurt you. What did you think he was going to do?

QUEEN.
I thought he was going to bite me!

ANDREW.
The mouse is more afraid of you than you are of it. I'll just put this green pea under the mattresses. That should do it.

QUEEN.
Yes, and just in time. Someone is at the door. How do I look? Do I look okay? How does the castle look?

ANDREW.
You look fine. The castle looks fine, too. It is clean and shiny, with no spider webs or bugs. I'll go see who is at the door. [*Andrew exits. Pick up a cockroach on a control stick and run it across the playboard, and then fly it at the queen.*]

QUEEN.
Help, help! There's a cockroach in here. He's dive-bombing me. Help, help!

[*Put the princess puppet on your left hand.*]

SARAH.
[*Sarah enters at stage left.*] Hello, Your Majesty. What seems to be the problem?

QUEEN.
Problem? Why, yes. I've got a problem. A big problem. You see, there's this big—aah, big bed here for someone who needs a place to sleep. I was just getting it ready. Who are you?

SARAH.
My name is Sarah. I'm a princess. I'm so tired from traveling.

QUEEN.
A real princess? [*Aside to the audience:*] We'll see about that. Can you believe that hair?

SARAH.
What did you say?

QUEEN.
I said, "I like your hair." We do have a place ready for you. I think you will be comfortable. Go ahead and climb in.

SARAH.

I can't climb up there. It's too high.

QUEEN.

I'll get Andrew to help you. Andrew, oh Andrew, where are you?" [*Queen exits.*]

ANDREW.

[*Andrew enters.*] Hello, my name is Andrew. I'm the prince at this castle.

SARAH.

My name is Sarah. I'm a princess.

ANDREW.

A real princess? Say, I've been looking for a princess. What do you like to do in your spare time?

SARAH.

I like to read books, ride horses, and travel.

ANDREW.

So do I. Mother said you needed help getting into bed. She really piled those mattresses up high. Let me help you. There, I hope you're comfortable. See you in the morning. [*Andrew helps push the princess on top of the mattresses and exits at stage left. Andrew reenters at stage left. Sarah and the mattresses remain onstage.*]

ANDREW.

Where is everybody? It's morning. Is she awake yet? I can't wait to see if she is a real princess. I think she will make a fine wife.

QUEEN.

[*Queen enters at stage right.*] Now, why would you say a thing like that?

ANDREW.

Mother, she likes to travel, she likes to read, and—

QUEEN.

You don't have time to travel. I want you to take me to the Cheapskate Club today. I want to buy a VCR. You will take me, won't you, Andrew? [*She slaps at herself.*] There's a mosquito in here. Andrew, get that mosquito. [*Queen and Andrew slap at the air and each other.*] I'll get some bug spray. [*Queen exits.*]

SARAH.

[*Sarah gets out of bed.*] What a terrible night! There must have been a rock in my bed. I didn't get any sleep at all.

ANDREW.

You are a real princess! Hooray! We can get married! Where do you want to travel? Have you been to Texas? [*They kiss and exit stage left.*]

QUEEN.

Andrew, come back here! Don't marry her. Now why would they want to go to Texas? Sakowitz! Don't take Sarah to Sakowitz. You'll be sorry. Stay here with me. Ooh, now who is going to take me to the Cheapskate Club? [*You may want to substitute a local place for the word* Texas *and a local department store for the word* Sakowitz.]

Sody Sallyraytus

SUBJECT: Folktales

BOOKS TO READ: Any folktale.

MATERIALS: Five small, cloth-stuffed people: mother, father, girl, boy, storekeeper; small squirrel figurine; hand puppet: bear with an opening in the mouth to enable it to swallow characters; recording: "Sody Sallyraytus" [e.g., *Tales to Grow On* by The Folktellers (Weston Woods, 1981), available on cassette from The Folktellers, P.O. Box 2898, Ashville, NC 28802; call (704) 258-1113; the folktales on this cassette are recorded in their native formats]; props: small rocking chair or store counter, small house or bench, a bridge; pair of black gloves; hand puppet stage.

SETUP: Place the chair or store counter on the playboard at stage right. Place the storekeeper in the chair or at the store counter. Place the house or bench on the playboard at stage left. Set the cloth-stuffed mother, father, boy, girl, and squirrel on the playboard at various places (such that you can reach them from behind the scrim). Place the bridge on the playboard close to the store setting.

THE SHOW

Start the recording. Put on the black gloves. The first character to appear is the mother. Move her according to the action in the story, turning her around and nodding her head as she speaks (to walk a figure across the playboard, grasp it around its waist with your thumb and forefinger). She sends the boy to the store for some sody sallyraytus, so walk him across the playboard, over the bridge, and up to the storekeeper.

When the storekeeper hands the boy a poke of sody sallyraytus, nothing is actually exchanged, but lean the two puppets toward each other. Press the rocking chair rockers down for a rocking motion. Do not take the storekeeper out of the chair.

Turn the boy around. Walk him across the bridge, and pop the bear's head up over the edge of the playboard. With your left hand in the bear's head, reach out toward the boy. With your right hand on the boy, push him into the bear's mouth, which has an opening at the back. Allow your left hand to grab the boy and pull him into the bear's body. Walk the bear offstage.

As the recording continues, repeat with each character in the same manner, leaving the characters inside the bear. Both hands are needed for character interaction, so take the bear off your hand after he exits the stage each time, until the mother character is swallowed. Leave the bear on your left hand at this point.

When the squirrel runs up a tree to escape the bear, hold the squirrel in your right hand, and raise your right arm until your elbow is resting on the playboard. Then inch the bear up your arm, and drop the bear on the playboard when the recording says that the branch broke and the bear fell.

Set the squirrel on the playboard. Pull the people out of the bear. Pick up the squirrel and run him home. Walk the other characters home. Pantomime the mother handing the squirrel some biscuits. Set her back down.

Come out from behind the stage and take a bow.

The Three Billy Goats Gruff

SUBJECT: Goats / Folktales

BOOKS TO READ:
    The Three Billy Goats Gruff by Paul Galdone (Clarion Books, 1973).
    The Queen's Goat by Margaret Mahy (Dial Books for Young Readers, 1991).

MATERIALS:
    Glove Puppet Presentation—Glove puppet (a pattern is provided on p. 74).
    Shadow Puppet Presentation—Four shadow puppets: troll, large goat, medium goat, small goat; bridge (see pp. 75–79 for puppet and bridge patterns); cardboard box (approximately 16 by 16 inches); white cloth (e.g., a sheet); tape or staples; light source (e.g., a tiny lamp that fits inside the box); four dowels.

SETUP:
    Glove Puppet Presentation—Make the glove puppet and place it on your left hand. You can stand or sit, facing your audience, for this presentation.
    Shadow Puppet Presentation—Cut the bottom out of the cardboard box and cover the opening with white cloth. Tape or staple the sheet in place. Turn the box on its side. There needs to be a light source behind the shadow puppets (I use a tiny lamp inside the box to get the shadow effect) and the room must be dark. Tape rods (e.g., dowels) to the shadow puppets.

THE SHOW

Glove Puppet Presentation

YOU.
Once upon a time, there were three billy goats who wanted to go up the hill to eat grass. The name of all three was Gruff. On the way up, they had to cross a bridge over a stream. Under the bridge lived a great ugly troll. First of all over the bridge came the youngest Billy Goat Gruff. Trip, trap, trip, trap went the bridge. [*Tap your forefinger (the black goat) against your pinkie finger (the bridge).*]

TROLL.
Who's that tripping over my bridge?! [*Wiggle your thumb and move it beneath your pinkie finger while the troll is talking beneath the bridge.*]

BLACK GOAT.
Oh, it is only I, the tiniest Billy Goat Gruff. I'm going up the hill to eat grass.

[*Wiggle your forefinger while the black goat is talking.*]

TROLL.
Now, I'm coming to gobble you up!

BLACK GOAT.
Oh no, don't take me, I'm too little, that I am. Wait a bit till the second Billy Goat Gruff comes. He's much bigger.

TROLL.
Well, be off with you.

YOU.
A little later, up came the second Billy Goat Gruff. Trip, trap, trip, trap, trip, trap went the bridge. [*Tap your middle finger (the tan goat) against your pinkie finger.*]

TROLL.
Who's that tripping over my bridge?!

TAN GOAT.

Oh, it's the second Billy Goat Gruff, and I'm going to the hillside to eat grass.[*Wiggle your middle finger while the tan goat is talking.*]

TROLL.

Now I'm coming to gobble you up!

TAN GOAT.

Oh no, don't take me. Wait till the Big Billy Goat Gruff comes. He's much bigger.

YOU.

Just then, up came the Big Billy Goat Gruff. Trip trap, trip, trap, trip, trap went the bridge. [*Tap your ring finger (the brown goat) against your pinkie finger.*]

TROLL.

Who's that tramping over my bridge?!

BROWN GOAT.

It's I, the Big Billy Goat Gruff. [*Wiggle your ring finger while the brown goat is talking.*]

TROLL.

Now I'm coming to gobble you up!

BROWN GOAT.

Well, come along! I've got two spears, and I'll poke your eyeballs out at your ears. I've got, besides, two great big stones, and I'll crush you to bits, body and bones!

YOU.

That was what the Big Billy Goat said. That is what he did. [*Troll (thumb) and largest goat (ring finger) smash into each other.*] Then the Big Billy Goat went up to the hillside with his brothers. There the Billy Goats Gruff got so fat eating grass they were scarcely able to walk home again. If the fat hasn't fallen off them—why, they're still fat; and so—snip, snap, snout, this tale's told out.

Shadow Puppet Presentation

Hold the shadow puppets up against the white cloth (outside the box) to achieve the best effect. When it is time for the troll to speak, hold him against the white cloth. As he lets each goat cross the bridge, remove the troll and move the goat across. For the ending, hold all three goats against the white cloth.

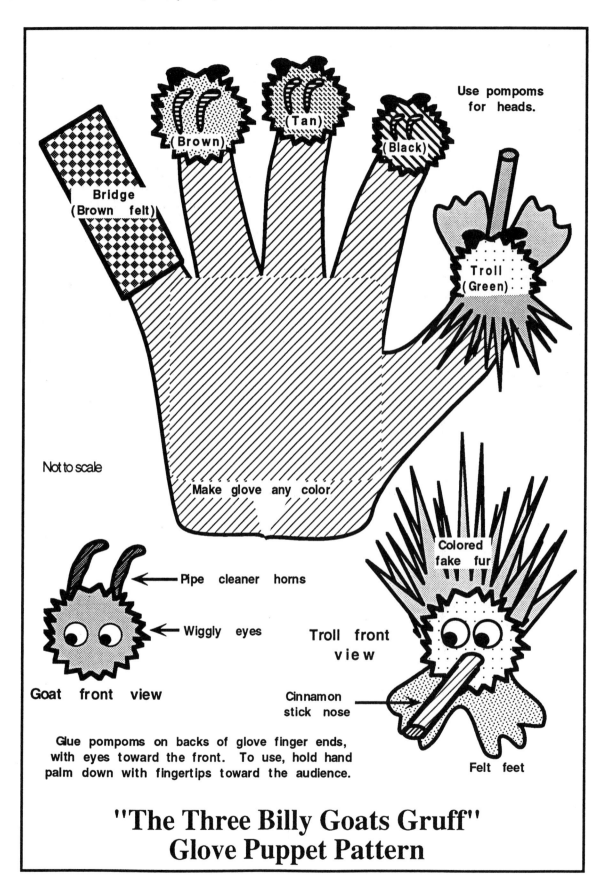

Use pompoms for heads.

Bridge
(Brown felt)

(Brown)

(Tan)

(Black)

Troll
(Green)

Not to scale

Make glove any color.

Colored fake fur

Pipe cleaner horns

Wiggly eyes

Goat front view

Troll front view

Cinnamon stick nose

Felt feet

Glue pompoms on backs of glove finger ends, with eyes toward the front. To use, hold hand palm down with fingertips toward the audience.

"The Three Billy Goats Gruff"
Glove Puppet Pattern

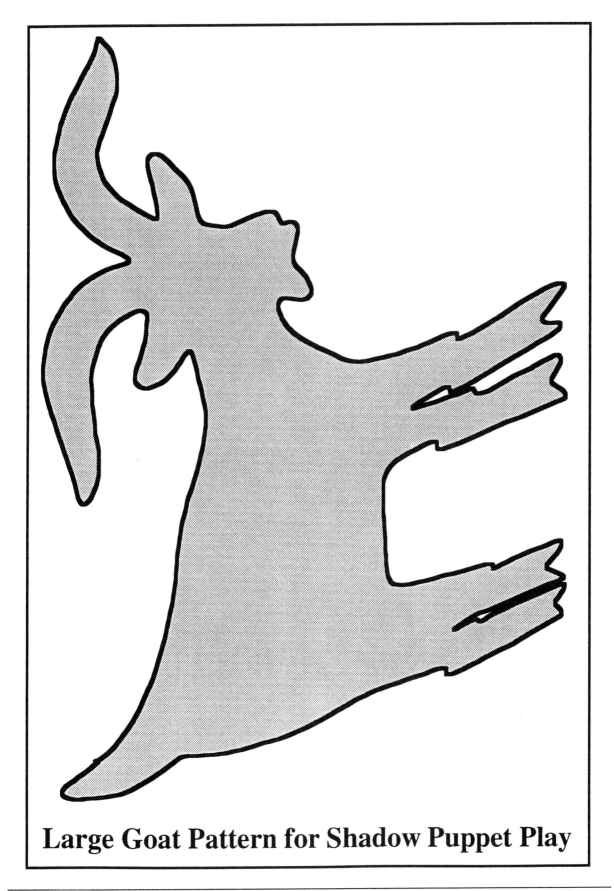

Large Goat Pattern for Shadow Puppet Play

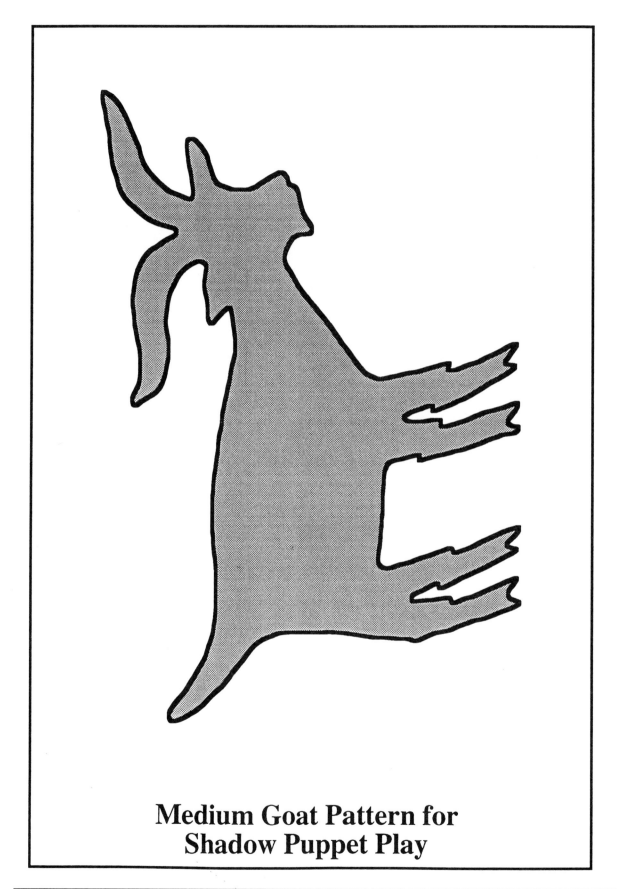

Medium Goat Pattern for
Shadow Puppet Play

Small Goat Pattern for Shadow Puppet Play

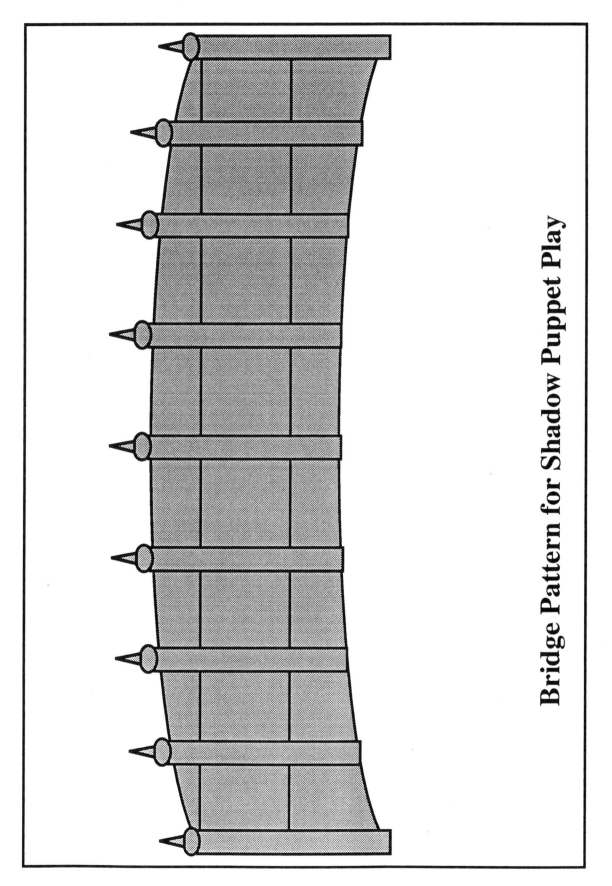

Bridge Pattern for Shadow Puppet Play

Troll Pattern for Shadow Puppet Play

The Three Little Pigs

SUBJECT: Weather / Pigs / Folktales

BOOKS TO READ:
> *Cloudy with a Chance of Meatballs* by Judith Barrett (Atheneum, 1978).
> *Julius* by Angela Johnson (Orchard Books, 1993).
> *The True Story of the Three Little Pigs* by Jon Scieska (Viking, 1989).

MATERIALS: Glove puppet (dark-colored felt, needle, thread, three small pink pompoms, one large brown pompom, wiggly eyes, glue, needle, thread).

SETUP: On a piece of felt, trace your right hand with your fingers spread apart. Cut out this pattern on two pieces of felt, simultaneously. Sew the two pieces of felt together. Sew the pompoms to the fingertips of the glove (the pink pompoms go on the pinkie, ring, and middle fingers; the brown pompom goes on the forefinger). Glue wiggly eyes on the pompoms.

THE SHOW

YOU.
Do you know the story of the three little pigs? You do? Well, I think I do, too. If I get mixed up, will you help me? Okay.

Once upon a time three little pigs went out into the world. They each built a nice house. The first little pig built a yellow house. It was made of banana Popsicles.

CHILDREN.
No! [*Then they say:*] Straw and hay.

YOU.
Oh, yeah. It was yellow straw, not yellow banana Popsicles.

WOLF.
Knock, knock, knock. [*As you speak, bend your forefinger (the wolf) up and down.*] Let me in.

PIG.
Not by the hair of my chinny chin chin. [*As you speak, bend your pinkie finger (the first pig) up and down.*]

WOLF.
Then I'll huff, and I'll puff, and I'll blow your house in. [*As you speak, bend your forefinger up and down.*]

YOU.
So the wolf huffed, and he puffed, and he quickly blew that straw house down. The little pig ran to the second little pig's house. Now, the second little pig had built a brown house, and it was made of Fudgesicles.

CHILDREN.
No! [*Then they say:*] Wood and twigs.

YOU.
Oh, yeah. It was brown twigs and sticks, not brown Fudgesicles.

WOLF.
Knock, knock, knock. [*As you speak, bend your forefinger up and down.*] Let me in.

PIG.
Not by the hair of my chinny chin chin. [*As you speak, bend your ring finger (the second pig) up and down.*]

WOLF.

Then I'll huff, and I'll puff, and I'll blow your house in. [*As you speak, bend your forefinger up and down.*]

YOU.

So the wolf huffed, and he puffed, and he barely blew that house down. The two little pigs ran to the third little pig's house. Now, the third little pig had built a pink house. It was made of Dreamsicles.

CHILDREN.

No! [*Then they say:*] Bricks.

YOU.

Oh, yeah. It was pink bricks, not pink Dreamsicles.

WOLF.

Knock, knock, knock. Let me in. [*As you speak, bend your forefinger up and down.*]

PIG.

Not by the hair of my chinny chin chin. [*As you speak, bend your middle finger (the third pig) up and down.*]

WOLF.

Then I'll huff, and I'll puff, and I'll blow your house in. [*As you speak, bend your forefinger up and down.*]

YOU.

The wolf drew his breath deeply and slowly as he huffed and he puffed, but he couldn't blow that house down. He decided to climb onto the roof and get inside the house by sliding down the chimney. Those pigs saw what he was going to do, and they put a big pot of hot chocolate on the fire.

CHILDREN.

No! [*Then they say:*] Hot boiling water.

YOU.

He didn't get any hot chocolate? I thought he was going to ask for marshmallows to go with the hot chocolate! The wolf quietly climbed onto the roof. [*Point your forefinger straight up.*] He quickly slid down the chimney. [*Bend your forefinger.*] When he landed in the boiling hot water he screamed, "Yyyeeeoooowww!" He made a rapid climb up the chimney. After a flying leap off the roof and a heavy landing on the ground, he ran so fast and so far that the three little pigs never saw that wolf again.

Thank you for helping me with the story.

The Tortoise and the Hare

SUBJECT: Aesop's Fables / Turtles

BOOKS TO READ:
> *I Can't Get My Turtle to Move* by Elizabeth Lee O'Donnell (Morrow Children's Books, 1989).

MATERIALS: Hand puppet: hare; rod puppet: tortoise (finger puppets could also be used; see p. 84 for finger puppet patterns); prop: papier-mâché tree or a drawing of a rock taped to a rod (or some other prop that can represent the finish line for the race); hand puppet stage.

SETUP: Place the "finish line" prop at stage right (if using a picture taped to a rod, attach the rod to the playboard using a broom handle holder). Read aloud one of the many versions of Aesop's fable "The Tortoise and the Hare."

THE SHOW

[*The hare and the tortoise enter at stage left.*]

HARE.

[*Hare speaks aggressively:*] Hey, I'm the fastest one you know, I'm the fastest in this here show. You want to race with me, the brain? Why, I'm even faster than a train.

TORTOISE.

[*Tortoise speaks passively:*] I've got four feet, just like you. I'll try them in this race, they will have to do.

HARE.

[*Hare speaks aggressively:*] This will be fun, I'll hardly have to run. Yeah, it won't take me much time—winning this race will be a crime. [*Hare races around the playboard several times.*] Whew! I'm tired, got time for a nap while he creeps along—he is such a sap! [*Exit hare to backstage and make snoring sounds.*]

TORTOISE.

[*Tortoise speaks passively:*] I know I can do it. [*Tortoise moves slowly across the stage as he talks.*] I can win this race, I can get through it. I'll put a smile on my face. Take one more step, just one more mile, just one more minute—now I can smile. [*Tortoise reaches the finish line.*]

HARE.

[*Hare enters at stage left and races to the finish line. He exclaims with surprise:*] How could you be here? You are so slow. I stopped to take a nap and you beat me out. That makes me angry and makes me pout. [*Exit hare at stage right and make loud crying sounds. Hare says (from offstage): "How could I let him beat me? How could I let him beat me?"*]

TORTOISE.

The moral of this story is "Slow and steady gets the job done."

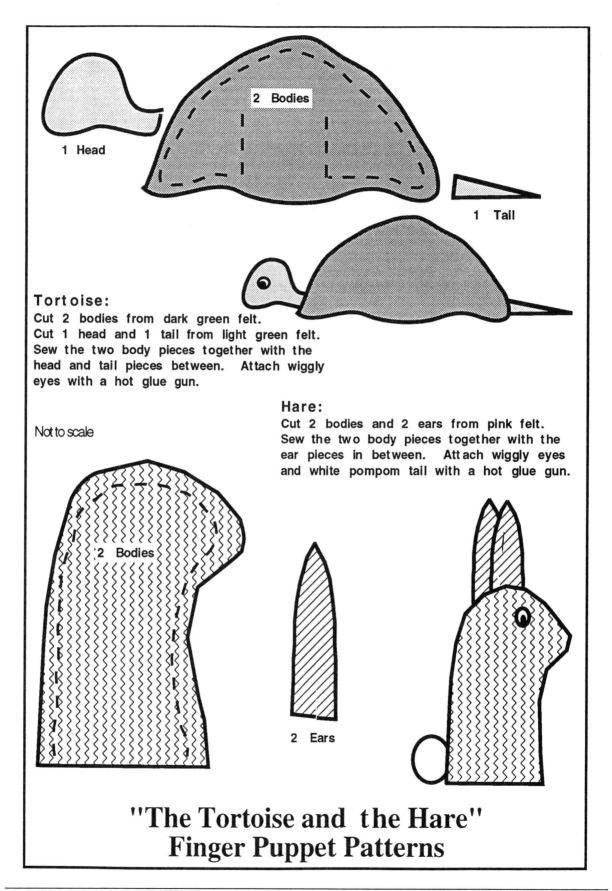

1 Head

2 Bodies

1 Tail

Tortoise:
Cut 2 bodies from dark green felt.
Cut 1 head and 1 tail from light green felt.
Sew the two body pieces together with the head and tail pieces between. Attach wiggly eyes with a hot glue gun.

Not to scale

Hare:
Cut 2 bodies and 2 ears from pink felt.
Sew the two body pieces together with the ear pieces in between. Attach wiggly eyes and white pompom tail with a hot glue gun.

2 Bodies

2 Ears

"The Tortoise and the Hare"
Finger Puppet Patterns

Part III

Songs,
Lyrics, and Rhymes

The Doggie in the Window

SUBJECT: Dogs / Pets

BOOKS TO READ:
Mine Will, Said John by Helen Griffith (Greenwillow Books, 1980).
What's Claude Doing? by Dick Gackenbach (Clarion Books, 1984).
Educating Arthur by Amanda Graham (Gareth Stevens, 1987).

MATERIALS: Hand puppet: dog with long legs; recording: "Doggie in the Window" [e.g., *The Patti Page Collection, Volume 2* (PolyGram Records, 1991), available on compact disc and cassette in music stores]; Velcro; props: short-sleeved pullover shirt, beach hat with elastic string. (No puppet stage is required.)

SETUP: This skit is perfect for the library story time subject of dogs. Using Velcro, fasten the dog's forelegs around your neck and the dog's hind legs around your waist. With the dog puppet on your right hand, hold the shirt and the beach hat in your left hand. Put the clothes in a place where you can reach them. Stand facing the audience.

THE SHOW

Start the recording of "Doggie in the Window." Whenever the dog barks on the recording, the dog puppet barks. At each sound the dog puppet makes, look at the dog and then at the audience in disbelief.

Pick up the shirt and hold it up for the dog's approval. It nods. Pull the shirt over the dog's head. The dog's mouth grabs the neck area of the shirt and will not let go. Tug and fuss until he finally lets go, as you nearly fall over. Pull the dog's forelegs through the arm holes of the shirt. Then fasten the dog's forelegs around your neck with the Velcro. Parrot sounds and cat meowing sounds are mouthed by the dog puppet. After each animal sound the dog makes, the puppeteer and the dog look at each other and then at the audience with a questioning expression. Listen closely to the recording for cues.

Pick up the hat. Hold it up in front of the dog. It looks at the hat and nods. Pass the hat over its head near its mouth as a tease. Pass it over again. On the third pass, the dog grabs the hat in its mouth and shakes it as a dog would. Yank the hat out of the dog's mouth. The dog grabs the elastic loop that is hanging from the hat. Turn the dog's mouth toward the ceiling, so the hat is hanging from the dog. Swing the hat back and forth. Then, as your hand in the dog's mouth turns the dog's head right side up, twirl the hat up into the air and let it land on the dog's head. Adjust the hat with your free hand to let the puppet's eyes show.

Now you have time for one big dog-lick up the side of your face as you grimace. Then, hold the dog's face next to yours, smile, and bow as the recording ends. Exit the stage area.

Frosty the Snowman

SUBJECT: Snow / Winter

BOOKS TO READ:
The Snowy Day by Ezra Jack Keats (Viking, 1962).
It's Snowing. It's Snowing by Jack Prelutsky (Greenwillow Books, 1984).
Oh Snow by Monica Mayper (HarperCollins, 1991).

MATERIALS: Hand puppets: snowman wearing a scarf (or a stuffed toy snowman), elf with arms that can grasp a broom and a bucket handle; props: small broom, small bucket of plastic snow; recording: "Frosty the Snowman" [e.g., *Merry Christmas* by Joe Scruggs (Educational Graphics Press, 1989), available on compact disc, cassette, and LP from teacher supply stores and from the Educational Record Center, 3233 Burnt Mill Dr., Suite 100, Wilmington, NC 28403; call (800) 438-1637]; hand puppet stage.

SETUP: If you have purchased a stuffed toy snowman, remove some of the stuffing to make room for your hand.

THE SHOW

Start the recording. Put Frosty on your right hand. Bring the puppet onstage and waltz him all the way across the playboard, from your right to your left and then back across the stage.

Put the elf puppet on your left hand and bring him onstage at stage left. The elf grabs at Frosty's scarf. The elf exits the stage and comes back onstage with a bucket of snow. The elf dumps the snow on Frosty's head. The elf exits, leaves the bucket backstage, and returns with a small broom. Frosty continues to dance back and forth onstage, while the elf sweeps the snow away from Frosty and the stage.

At the line in the song that says Frosty went to the village square with a broomstick in his hand, the elf tucks the broomstick in Frosty's scarf. Be sure to stop Frosty's movements when the recording says, "He only paused a moment when he heard him holler 'stop.'"

Move Frosty and the broom across the stage next to the elf as if to shove the elf off the stage. Then transfer the broom from Frosty to the elf, and let the elf sweep Frosty clear over to the edge of the stage, almost to the point of falling off. The elf then tucks the broom back into Frosty's scarf and pulls on the end of the scarf, pulling Frosty offstage.

Grandma's Glasses

SUBJECT: Grandparents / Eyeglasses

BOOKS TO READ:
Arthur's Eyes by Marc Brown (Little, Brown, 1979).
Good Morning, Granny Rose by Warren Ludwig (G. P. Putnam's Sons, 1990).
Granpa by John Burningham (Crown, 1984).

MATERIALS: Large, full-bodied hand puppet: grandma; recording: "Grandma's Glasses" [e.g., *Fingerplay Fun!* (Activity Records, 1979), available on cassette and LP in teacher supply stores and from the Educational Record Center, 3233 Burnt Mill Dr., Suite 100, Wilmington, NC 28403; call (800) 438-1637].

SETUP: Manipulate the puppet with one of your hands in its head and your other hand in the puppet's hand.

THE SHOW

Start the recording of "Grandma's Glasses." Put the puppet on your hands—one into the head and one into the puppet's arm and hand. When the recording says, "Make a circle with your thumb and finger, and hold it in front of your eyes," do this with the puppet's hand, placing it in front of the puppet's eyes. When the recording says, "This is grandma's hat," put the puppet's hand on top of the puppet's head, and so on.

Encourage the children in the audience to make the same hand motions as the puppet.

The Hokey Pokey

SUBJECT: Manners / Dancing

BOOKS TO READ:
Do Your Ears Hang Low? by Tom Glazer (Doubleday, 1980).
Perfect Pigs by Marc Brown (Little, Brown, 1983).

MATERIALS: Marionette puppet; recording: "The Hokey Pokey." (No stage is required.)

SETUP: Directions for making a marionette puppet can be found in the appendix (see pp. 112–13).

THE SHOW

Play a recording of "The Hokey Pokey" and manipulate the marionette as suggested in the recording. "Put your left foot in, put your left foot out, put your left foot in, and shake it all about. Do the Hokey Pokey and turn your self around. That's what it's all about!"

Children enjoy being so close to a puppet. After the song, explain the proper way to introduce oneself. Then walk the marionette up to each child and introduce the marionette to the child. Extend the marionette's hand for a handshake. Remind the children that we shake hands with our right hand.

When the marionette's hands and head are about child-size, children tend to act as if the marionette has the same strength they have. They grab the hand of the marionette and shake vigorously. If you use a small marionette with tiny hands, the children will shake hands more gently. You may need to remind them to be careful. If this does not work, step between them and the marionette.

You might want to use the following sample introductions as an opportunity to discuss library manners, such as proper care of books and returning books on time. Sample introductions:

MARIONETTE. Hi, my name is Jack!

CHILD. Hi, my name is Alice.

MARIONETTE. Hi, Alice. It's nice to meet you.

This will help you learn the names of the children. The marionette can then say good-bye, wave good-bye, and walk away.

Hula Girl Dances

SUBJECT: Dancing / Hawaii

BOOKS TO READ:
> *Our Ballet Class* by Stephanie Sorine (Alfred A. Knopf, 1981).
> *My Ballet Class* by Rachel Isadora (Greenwillow Books, 1980).
> *Come Dance with Me* by Carol Nicklaus (Silver Press, 1991).

MATERIALS: Puppet: Hawaiian hula girl with a large mouth that opens and closes; recording: "Little Brown Gal" [e.g., *The Best of Alfred Apaka* (MCA, 1973), available on cassette and LP in music stores].

SETUP: Dress the puppet in a grass skirt and a bikini top. Attach a tropical flower to her hair. Attach control sticks to the wrists of the puppet. Listen to the song before beginning the performance so you can practice the necessary hand motions (this hula dance will be done with hand motions rather than footsteps). Put the puppet on your right hand and grasp the control sticks with your left hand.

THE SHOW

Make the appropriate hand motions to accompany the recording of the song "Little Brown Gal." As an optional activity, hand out scarves to children and have them perform a free-spirited dance to music.

Jingle Bell Rock

SUBJECT: Christmas

BOOKS TO READ:
Cowboy Night Before Christmas by James Rice (Pelican, 1990).
Merry Christmas, Thomas by A. Vesey (Little, Brown, 1986).
How Little Porcupine Played Christmas by Joseph Slate (Thomas Y. Crowell, 1982).

MATERIALS: Hand puppets and rod puppets (one puppet for each child) dressed in holiday fashions, with jingle bells attached; recording: "Jingle Bell Rock" [e.g., *Merry Christmas* by Joe Scruggs (Educational Graphics Press, 1989), available on compact disc, cassette, and LP in teacher supply stores and from the Educational Record Center, 3233 Burnt Mill Dr., Suite 100, Wilmington, NC 28403; call (800) 438-1637]. (No stage is required.)

SETUP: Sample hand puppet patterns are provided on pages 93–95.

THE SHOW

Give each child a puppet. As they put the puppets on their hands, tell them you want to hear the jingle bells ring. Start the recording of "Jingle Bell Rock." Watch the children smile with delight as they shake their puppets. Halfway through the recording, suggest that they may trade puppets if they wish. This gives them an opportunity to use another type of puppet or one they think is better than the one they are using.

The children do not use a stage to perform this skit but rather walk around, watching each other's puppets perform. When I first started using this idea, I did not have enough puppets for all the children, so I let a few perform at a time and passed the puppets on to a few more children after playing a short portion of the recording.

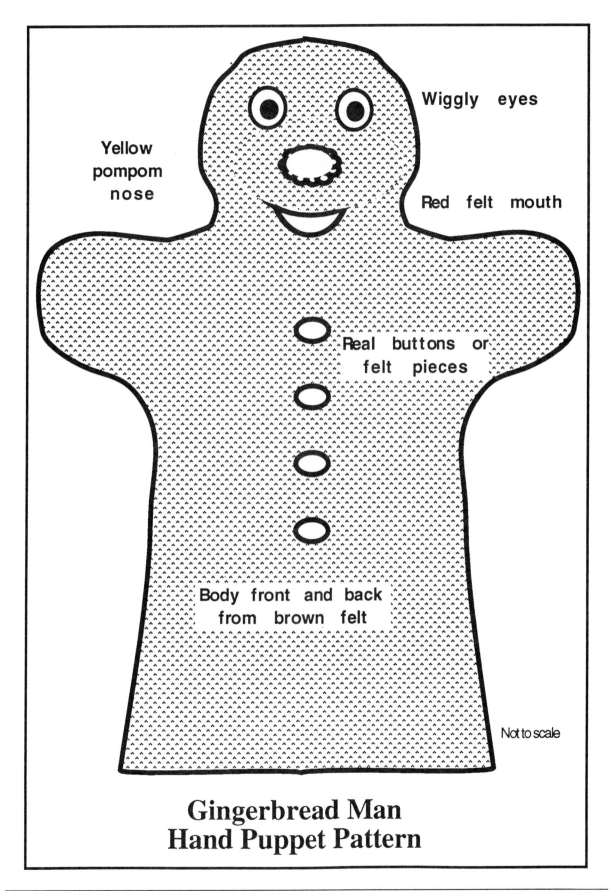

Wiggly eyes

Yellow
pompom
nose

Red felt mouth

Real buttons or
felt pieces

Body front and back
from brown felt

Not to scale

Gingerbread Man
Hand Puppet Pattern

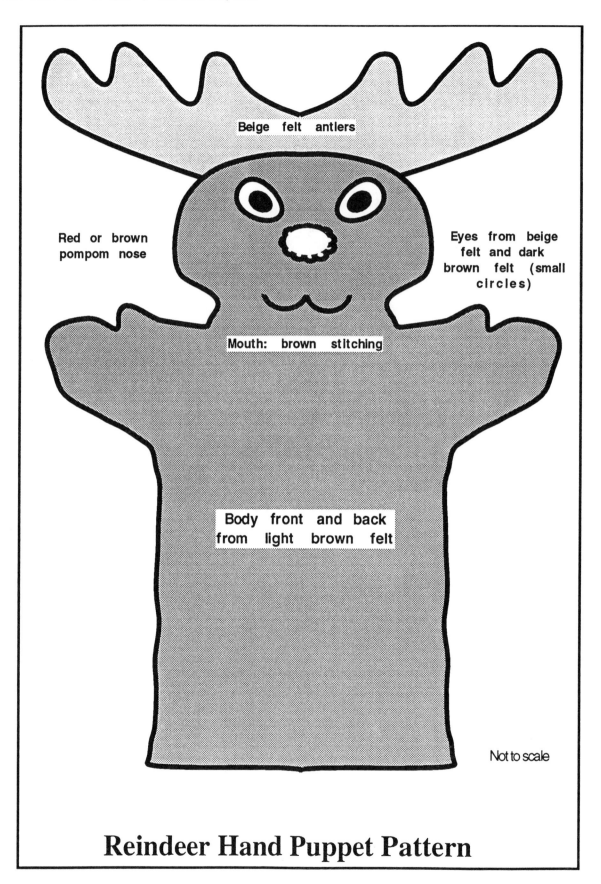

Beige felt antlers

Red or brown pompom nose

Eyes from beige felt and dark brown felt (small circles)

Mouth: brown stitching

Body front and back from light brown felt

Not to scale

Reindeer Hand Puppet Pattern

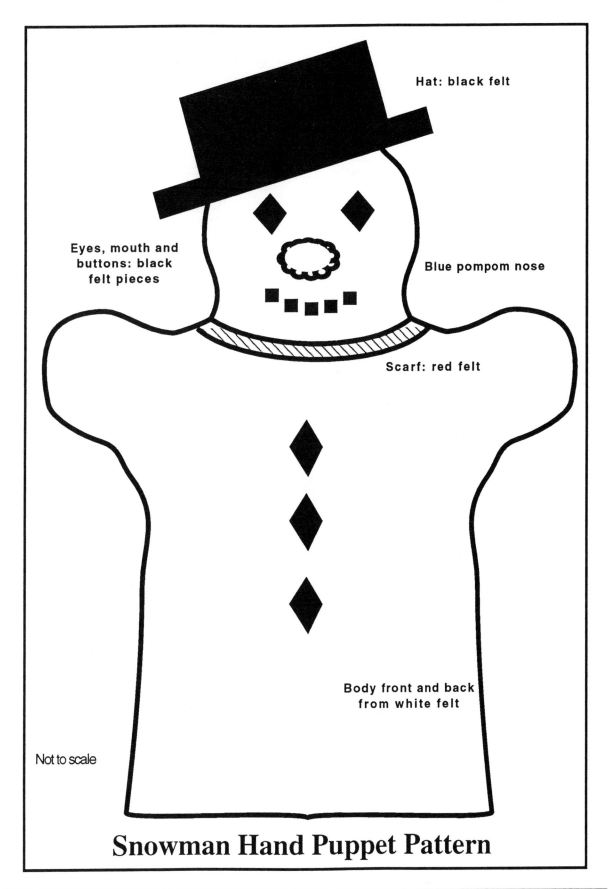

Hat: black felt

Eyes, mouth and buttons: black felt pieces

Blue pompom nose

Scarf: red felt

Body front and back from white felt

Not to scale

Snowman Hand Puppet Pattern

Miss Lucy Had a Baby

SUBJECT: Babies

BOOKS TO READ:
> *Where's the Baby?* by Pat Hutchins (Greenwillow Books, 1988).
> *The Wild Baby* by Barbro Lindgren (Greenwillow Books, 1981).
> *Our Teacher's Having a Baby* by Eve Bunting (Clarion Books, 1992).

MATERIALS: Stuffed toy rabbits: Miss Lucy, Baby, lady with a purse; stuffed toy rats: nurse, doctor; prop: toy baby carriage (just big enough for Baby); green felt; hot glue gun and glue sticks; four dowels; hand puppet stage.

SETUP: Cut out a tiny felt alligator and glue it to the lady's purse. Hot-glue the dowels to the back of each character except Baby. Place Baby in the carriage, and place the carriage on the playboard at stage right.

THE SHOW

[Bring Miss Lucy onstage with your right hand. Walk her to Baby and stand her at the right side of the crib. Sing:]

Miss Lucy had a baby.
She named him Tiny Tim.
She put him in the bathtub
To see if he could swim.

He drank up all the water. *[Walk Miss Lucy to the other side of the carriage.]*
He ate up all the soap.
He tried to eat the bathtub,
But it wouldn't go down his throat.
[Walk Miss Lucy to the right side of the carriage.]

He floated up the river.
He floated down the lake.
And now Miss Lucy's baby
Has got a bellyache.

Miss Lucy called the doctor.

YOU.
[*Yell:*] Hey, Doc! *[Pick up Doctor with the left hand and walk him onstage from the left.]*

DOC.
Yes, what is it?

MISS LUCY.
It's the baby. He's got a bellyache.

DOC.
Hmm. I'll have to take a look. *[Move Doctor next to Miss Lucy and transfer his rod from your left hand to your right hand.]*

YOU.
[*Sing:*] "Miss Lucy called the nurse."
[*Yell:*] Hey, Nurse! *[Pick up Nurse with the left hand and walk her onstage from the left.]*

NURSE.
Yes, what is it?

MISS LUCY.
It's the baby. He's got a bellyache.

NURSE.
Hmm. I'll have to take a look. [*Move Nurse over to look at Baby. Transfer her rod from your left hand to your right hand. You will be holding three rods in your right hand at this point.*]

YOU.
[*Sing:*] "Miss Lucy called the lady with the alligator purse." [*Yell:*] Hey, Lady! [*Bring Lady with the alligator purse onstage with your left hand.*]

LADY.
Yes, what is it?

MISS LUCY.
It's the baby. He's got a bellyache.

LADY.
Hmm. I'll have to take a look. [*Move Lady over to look at Baby.*]

[*As each character talks in the upcoming dialog, move the character in some fashion so the audience will know who is talking. Try to give each character a different and distinct voice.*]

DOC.
I think he has the measles.

NURSE.
I think he has the mumps.

LADY.
I think he has a virus.

DOC.
What he needs is a shot of penicillin.

NURSE.
Oh, he just needs some bed rest.

LADY.
Are you kiddin'? What this kid needs is some pizza.

DOC.
Well, he'll live.

NURSE.
Yeah, he'll be all right.

LADY.
Well, I'm leaving.

NURSE.
So am I.

DOC.
Wait for me.

[*Move them all offstage to your left with your left hand. Move Miss Lucy from one side of the baby carriage to the other side as you sing:*]

Miss Lucy gave me peaches.
And then she gave me pears.
And then she gave me 50 cents,
And kicked me up the stairs.
My mother was born in England.
My father was born in France.
And I was born in diapers,
Because I had no pants.

[*Miss Lucy bows and exits stage left, with Baby in the carriage. Your left hand removes the carriage and your right hand removes Miss Lucy.*]

The Old Lady Who Swallowed a Fly

SUBJECT: Food

BOOKS TO READ:
>*Gregory the Terrible Eater* by Mitchell Sharmat (Four Winds Press, 1980).
>*Pancakes, Pancakes* by Eric Carle (Picture Book Studio, 1990).
>*If You Give a Mouse a Cookie* by Laura Joffe Numeroff (Harper & Row, 1985).

MATERIALS: Hand puppet: old lady; finger puppets: fly, spider, bird, cat, dog, cow, goat, horse.

SETUP: Make the puppets (if desired, you may use cardboard animal cutouts in place of any or all of the finger puppets). Patterns for the cat, dog, and cow are provided with the skit "The Little Red Hen" (see pp. 54, 55, and 57). Patterns for the fly, spider, goat, and horse are provided on page 100. A hand puppet pattern is provided on pages 101–2.

THE SHOW

First, read aloud one of the titles listed in "Books to Read." Next, hold the old lady puppet on one hand. Sing the song (below) and insert the finger puppets or cardboard animals that come with the large puppet into her mouth at the appropriate times. As you sing the song, make swallowing sounds as each animal is being swallowed. Make loud sounds for each animal, such as meows or barks, just before the animal is swallowed. This shows emotion on the part of the animals and catches the imagination of the audience.

I know an old lady who swallowed a fly. I don't know why she swallowed that fly. Perhaps she'll die.

I know an old lady who swallowed a spider that wriggled, jiggled, and tickled inside her. She swallowed the spider to catch the fly. I don't know why she swallowed that fly. Perhaps she'll die.

Old lady puppet is available from Nancy Renfro Studios, P.O. Box 164226, Austin, TX 78716; call (800) 933-5512.

I know an old lady who swallowed a bird. How absurd to swallow a bird. She swallowed the bird to catch the spider that wriggled, jiggled, and tickled inside her. She swallowed the spider to catch the fly. I don't know why she swallowed that fly. Perhaps she'll die.

I know an old lady who swallowed a cat. Fancy that, to swallow a cat. She swallowed the cat to catch the bird. She swallowed the bird to catch the spider that wriggled, jiggled, and tickled inside her. She swallowed the spider to catch the fly. I don't know why she swallowed that fly. Perhaps she'll die.

I know an old lady who swallowed a dog. What a hog, to swallow a dog. She swallowed the dog to catch the cat. She swallowed the cat to catch the bird. She swallowed the bird to catch the spider that wriggled, jiggled, and tickled inside her. She swallowed the spider to catch the fly. I don't know why she swallowed that fly. Perhaps she'll die.

I know an old lady who swallowed a goat. She opened her throat and swallowed a goat. She swallowed the goat to catch the dog. She swallowed the dog to catch the cat. She swallowed the cat to catch the bird. She swallowed the bird to catch the spider that wriggled, jiggled, and tickled inside her. She swallowed the spider to catch the fly. I don't know why she swallowed that fly. Perhaps she'll die.

I know an old lady who swallowed a cow. I don't know how she swallowed a cow. She swallowed the cow to catch the goat. She swallowed the goat to catch the dog. She swallowed the dog to catch the cat. She swallowed the cat to catch the bird. She swallowed the bird to catch the spider that wriggled, jiggled, and tickled inside her. She swallowed the spider to catch the fly. I don't know why she swallowed that fly. Perhaps she'll die.

I know an old lady who swallowed a horse. She's dead, of course! So you can just kiss her good-bye. [*Make a loud kissing sound.*]

Use wiggly eyes for all puppets.

Goat

Cut four feet and two bodies from black felt. Cut two horns from white felt. Position feet and horns between body pieces as shown and stitch along dashed line. Attach a 7mm wiggly eye to each side of the goat's head with a hot glue gun.

Fly

Pompoms

fold

Cut two fly bodies out of dark blue felt and one fly wing out of light blue felt. Fold the wing piece in the middle where shown by the heavy dashed line and stitch it to the top of one of the body pieces along the light dashed line as shown. Stitch the two body pieces together and attach pompoms and wiggly eyes as shown, using a hot glue gun.

Horse

Cut two horse head pieces out of white felt, sandwich a piece of white fringe between them, and stitch along the dashed lines. Attach a wiggly eye to each side of the head with a hot glue gun.

Not to scale

Spider

Cut two feet, two eyebrows, and one nose from black felt. Cut two body pieces from any other color felt. Position feet between body pieces as shown and stitch along dashed line. Attach wiggly eyes, eyebrows, and nose with a hot glue gun.

Finger Puppet Patterns for "The Old Lady Who Swallowed a Fly"

Make puppet from brown paper grocery sack turned upside down.

Use approximately one yard of Jumbo Loopy Chenille to make the hair.

Tape pink paper over sack bottom and portion of side to make the face. Glue patterned cloth over lower part of sack side to make the dress.

Large wiggly eyes

Pink pompom nose

Tape a clear transparency sheet behind a hole cut into the sack's side for viewing the contents of the stomach.

Draw the mouth with a felt marker: Upper lip on sack bottom and bottom lip in matching position on sack side. Draw inside of mouth between upper and lower lips on sack side beneath the bottom with a pink felt marker. Above the bottom lip on sack side, cut a slot along sack fold through which animal puppets can be swallowed.

Sandwich pink paper arms and tan paper legs between dress and sack side.

Not to scale

Old Lady Hand Puppet Pattern

From *Fun Puppet Skits for Schools and Libraries.* © 1995. Teacher Ideas Press. (800) 237-6124.

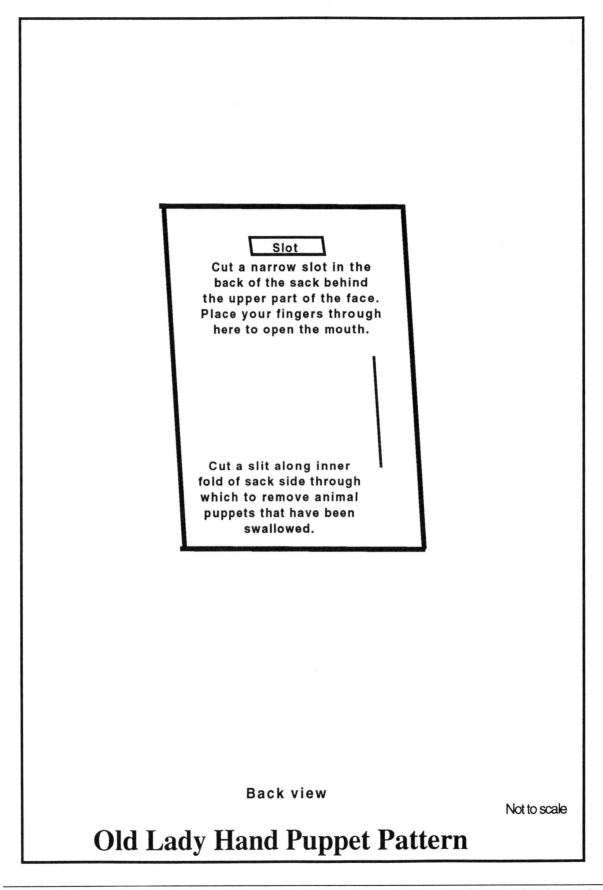

Slot

Cut a narrow slot in the
back of the sack behind
the upper part of the face.
Place your fingers through
here to open the mouth.

Cut a slit along inner
fold of sack side through
which to remove animal
puppets that have been
swallowed.

Back view

Not to scale

Old Lady Hand Puppet Pattern

Old MacDonald Had a Farm

SUBJECT: Farm Life / Animals

BOOKS TO READ:
The Ornery Morning by Patricia Brennan Demuth (Dutton Children's Books, 1991).
Once upon MacDonald's Farm . . . by Stephen Gammell (Four Winds Press, 1981).
Old MacDonald Had a Farm, illustrated by Lorinda Bryan Cauley (G. P. Putnam's Sons, 1989).

MATERIALS: Hand puppets to match the animals in the song (different versions of this song contain different animals; find one that you like and make or buy needed puppets accordingly); recording: "Old MacDonald Had a Farm" [e.g., *Rima Corral Sings Mother Goose Songs* (Rimco Records, 1992), available on cassette in teacher supply and music stores; the cassette includes English and Spanish versions, as well as an instrumental sing-along version]; a "barn" bag to hold all the animal puppets for this skit.

SETUP: Make the puppets (a pattern for a turkey hand puppet is provided on p. 104). Children enjoy being the performers in this skit. Give a puppet to each child and explain what you want the child to do as they hear the sound their animal puppet would make (e.g., for a dog puppet, make a barking sound and move the dog's mouth).

THE SHOW

Start the recording. As the song progresses, look at those children who are supposed to be manipulating their puppets. Give them reassurance by telling them they are doing a good job. Give them further directions by showing them how to hold their hand and arm. Lead them away from someone or something their puppet is biting.

At the end of the song, tell everyone to take a bow. As the children take the puppets off their hands, bring out the barn bag and let them put their puppets back in the bag.

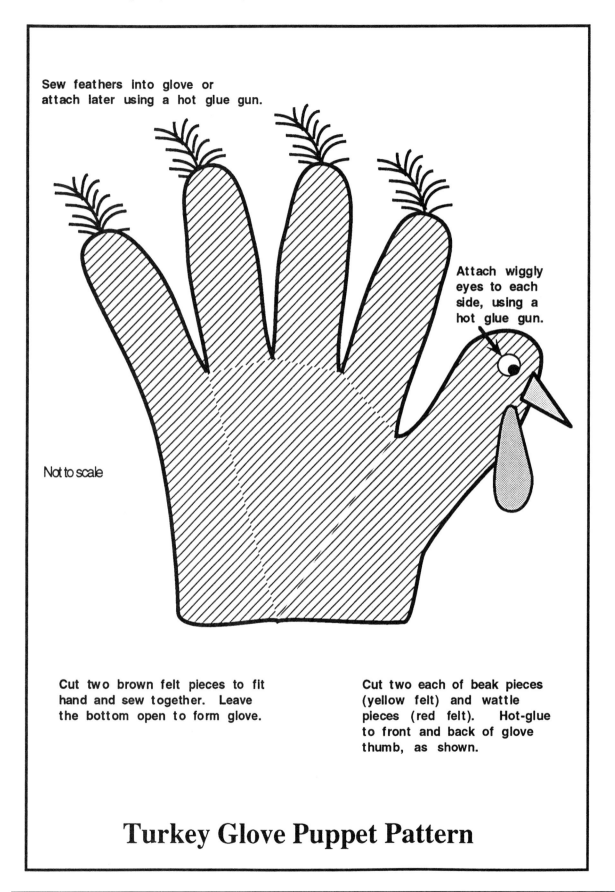

Sew feathers into glove or attach later using a hot glue gun.

Attach wiggly eyes to each side, using a hot glue gun.

Not to scale

Cut two brown felt pieces to fit hand and sew together. Leave the bottom open to form glove.

Cut two each of beak pieces (yellow felt) and wattle pieces (red felt). Hot-glue to front and back of glove thumb, as shown.

Turkey Glove Puppet Pattern

Old Mother Hubbard

SUBJECT: Mothers / Dogs

BOOKS TO READ:
> *The Last Puppy* by Frank Asch (Simon & Schuster, 1980).
> *Tallyho, Pinkerton!* by Steven Kellogg (Dial Books for Young Readers, 1982).
> *It Was Jake* by Anita Jeram (Little, Brown, 1991).

MATERIALS: Hand puppets: grandmother, dog with a mouth that opens and closes (a rod puppet could also be used for the grandmother); prop: tobacco pipe or pipe prop; hand puppet stage.

SETUP: Have the tobacco pipe or pipe prop nearby offstage.

THE SHOW

[*When the narrative begins, Old Mother Hubbard and the dog are at center stage. When you say the word* back *(as in "when she came back"), walk Mother Hubbard back to center stage.*]

YOU.

Old Mother Hubbard went to her cupboard to fetch her poor dog a bone. [*Mother Hubbard walks to one side of the stage, where she looks in her imaginary cupboard and shakes her head "no."*] But when she got there, the cupboard was bare, and so her poor dog had none. [*Mother Hubbard returns to center stage, where she again shakes her head "no."*]

DOG.

[*Dog howls a loud, mournful, "Ooooooo."*]

YOU.

She went to the baker's to buy him some bread. [*Mother Hubbard walks to one side of the stage to get the bread.*] And when she came back, the poor dog was dead. [*Mother Hubbard walks back to the dog, and shakes her head.*]

DOG.

[*Dog flips over on his back—drop him on the playboard with his mouth open, and yell, "Conk!"*]

YOU.

She went to the undertaker's to buy him a coffin. [*Mother Hubbard walks to one side of the stage.*] And when she came back, the poor dog was laughing. [*Mother Hubbard walks back to center stage.*]

DOG.

[*Dog sits up and looks at Mother Hubbard.*] I was just fooling, ha ha!

YOU.

She took a clean dish to get him some tripe. [*Mother Hubbard walks to one side of the stage.*] And when she came back, he was smoking a pipe. [*Mother Hubbard walks back to center stage.*]

DOG.

[*Dog puffs on the pipe.*]

YOU.

She went to the fishmonger's to buy him some fish. [*Mother Hubbard walks to one side of the stage.*] And when she came back, he was licking the dish. [*Mother Hubbard walks back to center stage.*]

DOG.

[*Dog makes licking, slurping sounds as he licks the playboard.*]

YOU.

She went to the fruiterer's to buy him some fruit. [*Mother Hubbard walks to one side of the stage.*] And when she came back, he was playing a flute. [*Mother Hubbard walks back to center stage.*]

DOG.

Tootle de toot de toot.

YOU.

She went to the tailor's to buy him a coat. [*Mother Hubbard walks to one side of the stage.*] And when she came back, he was riding a goat. [*Mother Hubbard walks back to center stage.*]

DOG.

[*Dog jumps around.*] Giddyap, giddyap, giddyap.

YOU.

She went to the hatter's to buy him a hat. [*Mother Hubbard walks to one side of the stage.*] And when she came back, he was feeding the cat. [*Mother Hubbard walks back to center stage.*]

DOG.

[*Dog looks around.*] Here kitty kitty, here kitty kitty, here kitty kitty.

YOU.

She went to the barber's to buy him a wig. [*Mother Hubbard walks to one side of the stage.*] And when she came back, he was dancing a jig. [*Mother Hubbard walks back to center stage.*]

DOG.

[*Flip the puppet's ears.*] Do de do de do.

YOU.

She went to the cobbler's to buy him some shoes. [*Mother Hubbard walks to one side of the stage.*] And when she came back, he was reading the news. [*Mother Hubbard walks back to center stage.*]

DOG.

It says here that there is going to be a puppet show today. Hey, I want to see it, too.

YOU.

She went to the hosier's to buy him some hose. [*Mother Hubbard walks to one side of the stage.*] And when she came back, he was trying on clothes. [*Mother Hubbard walks back to center stage.*]

DOG.

I can't find my pants.

YOU.

The dame made a curtsey. The dog made a bow. The dame said, "Your servant!" The dog said, "Bow-wow!" [*Puppets perform these motions as you recite these last lines.*]

The Twist

SUBJECT: Halloween / Costume Design / Monsters

BOOKS TO READ:
Halloween Monster by Catherine Stock (Bradbury Press, 1990).
Arthur's Halloween Costume by Lillian Hoban (Harper & Row, 1984).
Scary, Scary Halloween by Eve Bunting (Clarion Books, 1986).

MATERIALS: Hand puppets: baby, mother, three additional hand puppets (any desired characters); props: small bed that fits on the playboard, felt Halloween masks for the three additional puppets (e.g., an orange jack-o'-lantern mask), small monster mask on a stick; recording: "The Twist" by Chubby Checker [e.g., *Let's Twist* (K-tel International, 1994), available on compact disc and cassette at music stores]; hand puppet stage.

SETUP: Place the bed on the playboard at stage right. You will need to practice the entire pantomime a few times to get the timing right, so that the show ends at the end of the recording (when the music ends, the baby is back in bed—the party has ended, the identities of the partygoers have been revealed, and the partygoers have left). Put the mother hand puppet on your left hand. Put the baby hand puppet on your right hand.

THE SHOW

MOTHER.
[*Mother enters at stage left, carrying the baby hand puppet (which is on your right hand). The mother places the baby down on the bed.*] Now you have a good nap. Your daddy is sleeping and I will be right outside. [*She exits at stage left.*]

[*Your right hand is still in the baby puppet. Start the recording of "The Twist" with your foot or left hand. Bring the baby up out of bed and start him dancing the twist by rotating your hand right and left. Slip one of the costumed puppets onto your left hand, enter at stage left, and dance with the baby. Then exit the costumed puppet, slip it off your hand, put on another costumed puppet, and bring it onstage to dance with the baby. Do this also with the third costumed puppet and exit.*]

[*Now start all over. This time the baby dances with the character briefly and then tries to take the character's mask off. The baby grabs at the mask until he pulls it off to reveal who is behind the mask. That character exits, and you bring the next character onstage for the same kind of action. Continue this action until the three characters have been onstage and had their faces revealed to the audience. Put the baby back in bed. By this time the recording should have ended.*]

MOTHER.
[*Mother puppet enters on stage left to check on the baby. She walks over and looks at him.*] What a nice, quiet, sweet baby he is. [*She exits at stage left.*]

[*Take the mother puppet off your hand. Pick up a monster mask and bring it up to the side of the bed. As you lift the baby up from the bed, slide the mask up to cover his face. The mask should be on a long stick so your hand does not show as you hold the mask in front of the baby's face. The baby bows and exits with the monster mask in front of his face.*]

Appendix

Rod Puppet with Papier-Mâché Head

MATERIALS: Three-inch Styrofoam ball, dowel, brown paper sacks, wallpaper paste, gesso, acrylic paints, small paintbrushes (any kind), square of fabric, wiggly eyes, red or pink felt, yarn or wig hair, hot glue gun and glue sticks.

DIRECTIONS:

1. Tear the grocery bags into strips. Dip the strips into wallpaper paste and apply them to the ball. Cover the entire ball.

2. Form a nose, eye sockets, and a curved ridge for a mouth using strips dipped in wallpaper paste.

3. Rub the head down with wallpaper paste until it is smooth. Let dry.

4. Add a second layer of strips dipped in wallpaper paste. Let dry.

5. Paint the head with a layer of Gesso. Let dry.

6. Paint the head using acrylic paint. Let dry.

7. Now the puppet is ready for the finishing touches, such as hair, wiggly eyes, and a mouth cut from red or pink felt. Use a hot glue gun to apply these items. A square of fabric draped over the craft stick (the puppet's neck) will serve as clothes.

8. Push the draped craft stick up into the puppet head, and the puppet is ready to use.

Grasp the stick with your third, fourth, and fifth fingers, leaving your thumb and forefinger free to pick up objects. Your thumb and forefinger are the puppet's arms. Rod puppets with papier-mâché heads make excellent "people" puppets, which can be used in skits such as "Adventures in Baby-Sitting," "Claude the Dog," "The Gingerbread Boy," "Jingle Bell Rock," "The Library Is Closed," "Miss Lucy Had a Baby," "The Nutcracker and the Mouse King," and "The Princess and the Pea."

Rod Puppet with Styrofoam-Ball Head

MATERIALS: Three-inch-diameter Styrofoam ball, pompom, wiggly eyes, dowel, red or pink felt, yarn or wig hair, square piece of fabric, ribbon/trim or an artificial flower, hot glue gun and glue sticks.

DIRECTIONS:

1. (Optional) For black light use, spray paint the puppet with fluorescent paint. Try using one color on the head, another color on the yarn hair, and another on the clothing. You can also use fabric that responds well to black light. (Note: the spray painting should be done before assembling the puppet and before adding any ribbon, trim, or flowers.)

2. Choose a square of fabric for the dress or shirt. With a craft stick in your right hand, drape the fabric over the craft stick, with the end of the stick in the center of the fabric. Push the stick into a Styrofoam ball. The fabric and the stick form the body of the puppet, and the ball is the head.

3. Select wiggly eyes, a pompom nose, and a felt mouth. Use a hot glue gun to apply them to the ball.

4. If using hair from a wig, cut a small section of hair by cutting the fabric base to which the hair is attached. Glue this section onto the Styrofoam ball. Otherwise, glue on pieces of yarn.

5. Add ribbon, trim, or an artificial flower to your puppet to give it a personality.

Hold the puppet by grasping the stick under the fabric with your third, fourth, and fifth fingers. Your forefinger and thumb are the puppet's arms. This puppet may be used in the skits "Adventures in Baby-Sitting," in which the girl puppet must pick up the yarn-doll puppet (the fabric covers your entire hand as you manipulate the puppet), and "Old Mother Hubbard." Other skits using rod puppets include "Claude the Dog," "Don't Bother Me!," "Miss Lucy Had a Baby," and "The Nutcracker and the Mouse King."

Monster Sock Puppet

MATERIALS: Sock, wiggly eyes, 12-inch jumbo chenille stems or pipe cleaners, feathers, corks, felt, pompoms, plastic egg (such as the kind pantyhose are packed in), sequins, small Styrofoam balls, buttons, hot glue gun and glue sticks.

DIRECTIONS:

1. Select the desired materials to decorate your monster in a creative fashion.

2. Hot-glue the items onto the sock.

3. Drill two holes in one half of the plastic egg. Insert chenille stems or pipe cleaners for antennae or horns.

Slip your hand into the sock to manipulate the puppet. The monster puppet can be used in the skits "Adventures in Baby-Sitting," "Don't Bother Me!," and "The Twist." The making of this puppet is limited only by the imagination and the materials at hand. Have fun with it!

Dog Sock Puppet

MATERIALS: Sock, pompom, wiggly eyes, red or pink felt, brown or black, a piece of fake fur, hot glue gun and glue sticks.

DIRECTIONS:

1. Fold the toe seam in the sock to form the dog's mouth, with one end of the seam at the top of his mouth and the other end of the seam at the bottom of his mouth (the entire toe seam is on the inside of the dog's mouth).

2. Use a hot glue gun to attach a red or pink felt tongue to the dog's mouth (the tongue should hang out of the dog's mouth).

3. With hot glue, attach a pompom nose, wiggly eyes, brown or black felt ears (make them "floppy"), and a piece of fake fur as a topknot (at the top of the head between the ears).

Now your dog is ready to perform. This dog may be used in puppet skits such as "The City Mouse and the Country Mouse," "Claude the Dog," "The Gingerbread Boy," "The Little Red Hen," "Old MacDonald Had a Farm," and "Old Mother Hubbard."

Yarn Doll

MATERIALS: Yarn, 3-by-5-inch index card.

DIRECTIONS:

1. Wrap yarn around an index card (lengthwise) 20 times. Snip the coils of yarn along one edge of the index card. Holding the yarn together, slip the yarn off the card.

2. Grasp one end of the wrapped yarn as a doll head, and tie the head securely at the neck with a piece of yarn. Cut off the tie ends.

3. Place the yarn doll on a table, and separate out two or three strands of yarn on each side to form arms. Tie each arm in the middle and at the end with a piece of yarn.

4. Separate the remaining yarn strands into two legs. Tie them with yarn at the bottom to form legs.

This yarn doll may be used in the puppet skits "Adventures in Baby-Sitting" (in making and performing this skit, Brownie Scouts may earn a Try-It, fulfilling the requirements of making a yarn doll, making a hand puppet, making a rod puppet, and performing a short puppet skit) and "Miss Lucy Had a Baby."

Wooden-Spoon Marionette Puppet

MATERIALS: Wooden spoon, two wooden thread spools, two 10-inch lengths of heavy ribbon, square piece of cloth for the dress, fake fur for the hair, hair ribbon, two wiggly eyes, black marking pen, pink marking pen, two beads for earrings, pipe cleaner, two 1/4-inch dowels (9 inches and 12 inches long), 10-inch length of string, two 20-inch lengths of string, hot glue gun and glue sticks.

DIRECTIONS:

1. Drill a hole at the end of the cup of the spoon.

2. Tie the two 10-inch lengths of ribbon (the legs) to the end of the spoon handle (the spoon "form" is the puppet's head and body). Stuff the two loose ends of the ribbon into spools (the feet). Use hot glue to firmly attach the legs to the feet and the ribbons to the wooden spoon.

3. Tie the pipe cleaner (the arms) around the spoon handle. Use hot glue to firmly attach the arms to the spoon.

4. Wrap the piece of cloth (the dress) around the puppet's body and hot-glue into place.

5. Draw facial features on the spoon, using a black marking pen for features such as eyebrows, nose, and mouth, and a pink marking pen for the cheeks and lips.

6. Cut a piece of fake fur (the hair) and hot-glue it in place (do not cover the drilled hole). Attach the hair ribbon with hot glue.

7. Tie together and hot-glue the two 1/4-inch dowels to form a cross (the control bar; see p. 113). Tie the two 20-inch lengths of string to the arms of the control bar. Tie the other ends of these two 20-inch lengths of string to the knees of the puppet. Tie the 10-inch length of string to the hole drilled in the spoon cup. Tie the other end of the 10-inch length of string to the middle of the 12-inch dowel on the control bar (adjust the string length so that the puppet stands upright).

8. Hot-glue a piece of fake fur over the hole in the spoon.

Marionette manipulation is quite easy once you understand how a movement of the control bar corresponds to a movement by the puppet. To control the feet and make the puppet walk and dance, the strings are attached to the puppet's knees. By raising the foot control bar at one end, the attached leg will rise. Alternate raising and lowering the ends of the foot bar, and the puppet walks. You must walk along with it, or it will just walk in place. Notice that when you raise your knee, your foot comes up. The same principle is used in making a marionette puppet walk. Marionettes are used in the skits "The Hokey Pokey" and "The Nutcracker and the Mouse King."

Drill a hole in the spoon "head" and fix a string from the control rod to the spoon.

The control rod is made of 1/4-inch diameter dowels. The center piece is 12 inches long and the cross piece is 9 inches long. Tie together with string and use hot glue.

Glue fur, ribbon, and two wiggly eyes to the head. Draw facial features with marking pens.

Use a wooden spoon for the body.

Use a piece of cloth wrapped around the spoon handle for the dress.

Use a thick pipe cleaner for the arms.

Use a heavy ribbon for the legs.

Strings from the ends of the control rod cross-piece attach to the knees of the puppet.

Use wooden thread spools for the feet.

Not to scale

Wooden-Spoon Marionette

Skit Subject Index

Author/Title Index

About the Author

Joanne Schroeder received her degree in education/library science from the University of Central Florida. She has worked as a children's librarian for a total of 22 years—in a public library, in elementary school libraries, and in a junior high school.

Working extensively with the Greater Houston Puppetry Guild, teaching and attending puppet workshops, and using puppetry in her job as a librarian have enabled Joanne to master the art of puppetry. She has directed puppet workshops at local, regional, and national puppet festivals.

Her puppet programs are especially well received at libraries and library conferences, as the emphasis is always on promoting reading. Puppeteers of America has selected Joanne to serve as the Library Consultant for their organization. She has received awards from the Houston and Dallas puppet guilds for her dedication to the art of puppetry. Fisher Elementary School in Pasadena, Texas awarded her an Honorary Life Membership in the Texas Congress of Parents and Teachers in recognition of her distinguished service to children.

Joanne lives in Friendswood, Texas with her husband Syd.